Collage Imagery

A Collection of
Photographic Images
for Use in Personal Art

Catherine Anderson

ISBN-13: 978-098852719
ISBN-10: 098852711

www.catherineandersonstudio.com

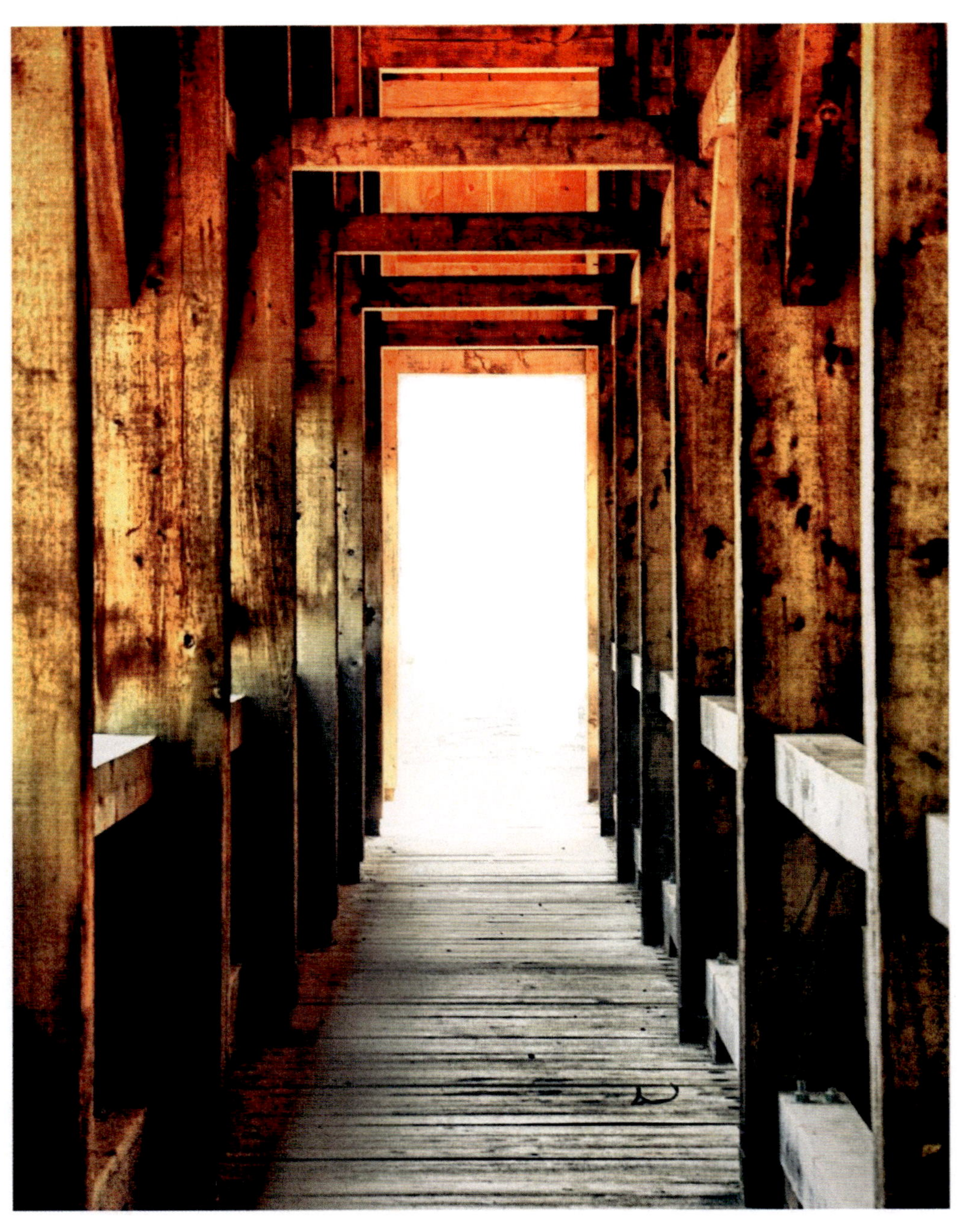

Dear Artist,

I originally created this collection of my photographs as a source of images to be freely used for the making of SoulCollage® cards. SoulCollage® is an intuitive, self-discovery process created by Seena Frost, author of *SoulCollage® Evolving*. It is a transformative and creative process, and one I have used for many years for my own personal growth. You can find out more about the process at www.soulcollage.com.

The SoulCollage® Facilitator community is an extremely generous one, where sharing of resources is at the heart of the community. This Facilitator community has inspired me to offer these images to you for your personal use in the hope that they might inspire you to create, whether that be on cards, journal pages or collage art.

You could also use these photographs as visual journal prompts for writing. The book can be cut up and the images kept in a box so you can intuitively choose an image and let it take you on a journey of imagination and inspiration.

By printing the images in this book format, the cost per page is less than the cost of a color copy, and much less than the cost of printing a page on your personal computer.

You have my permission and encouragement to cut out the images in this book and use them freely for making SoulCollage® cards, collage art, art journal pages or in craft projects, and to share your creations on your website, blog, or in social media.

Have fun collaging and creating!

Creative blessings,
Catherine

www.catherineandersonstudio.com

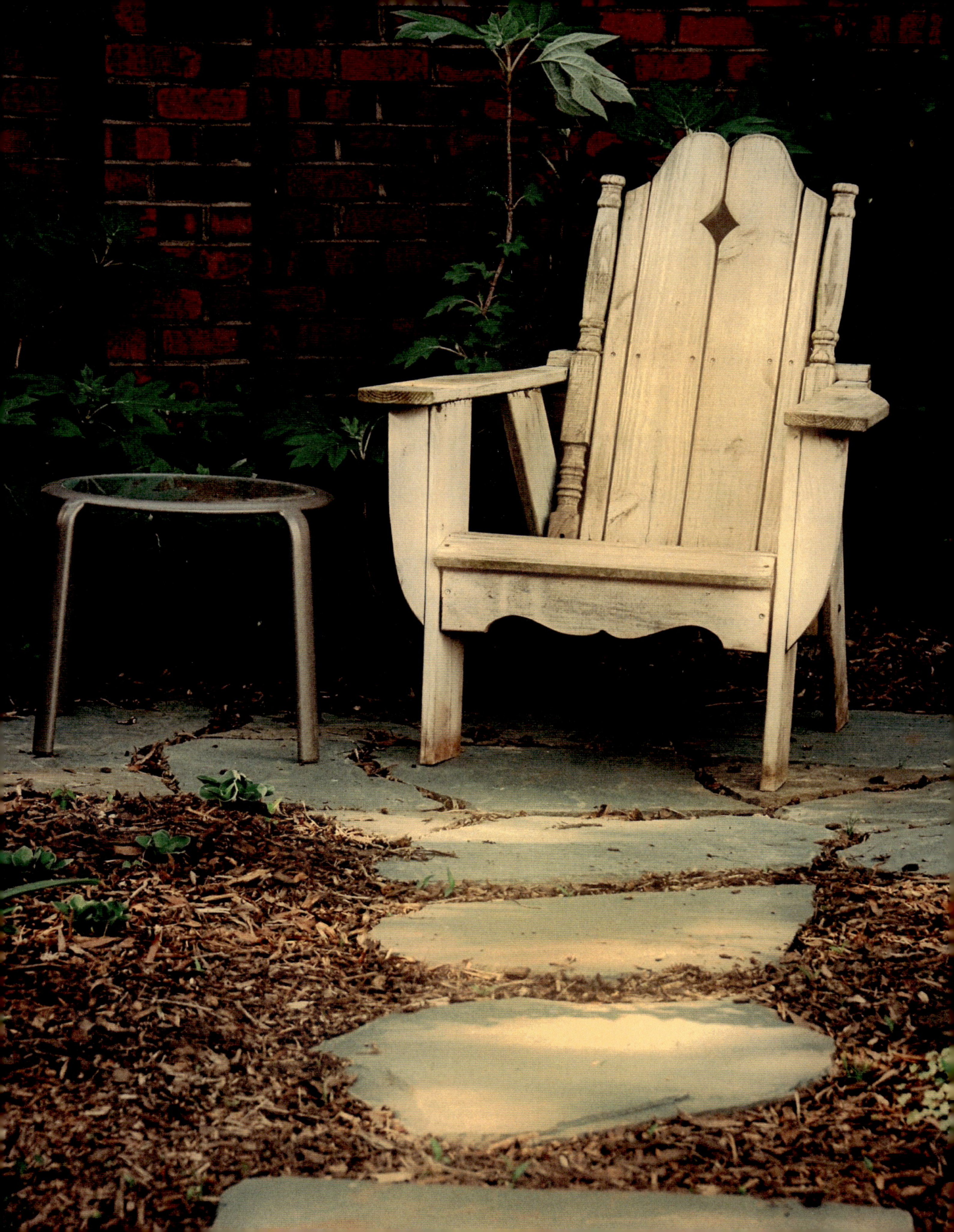

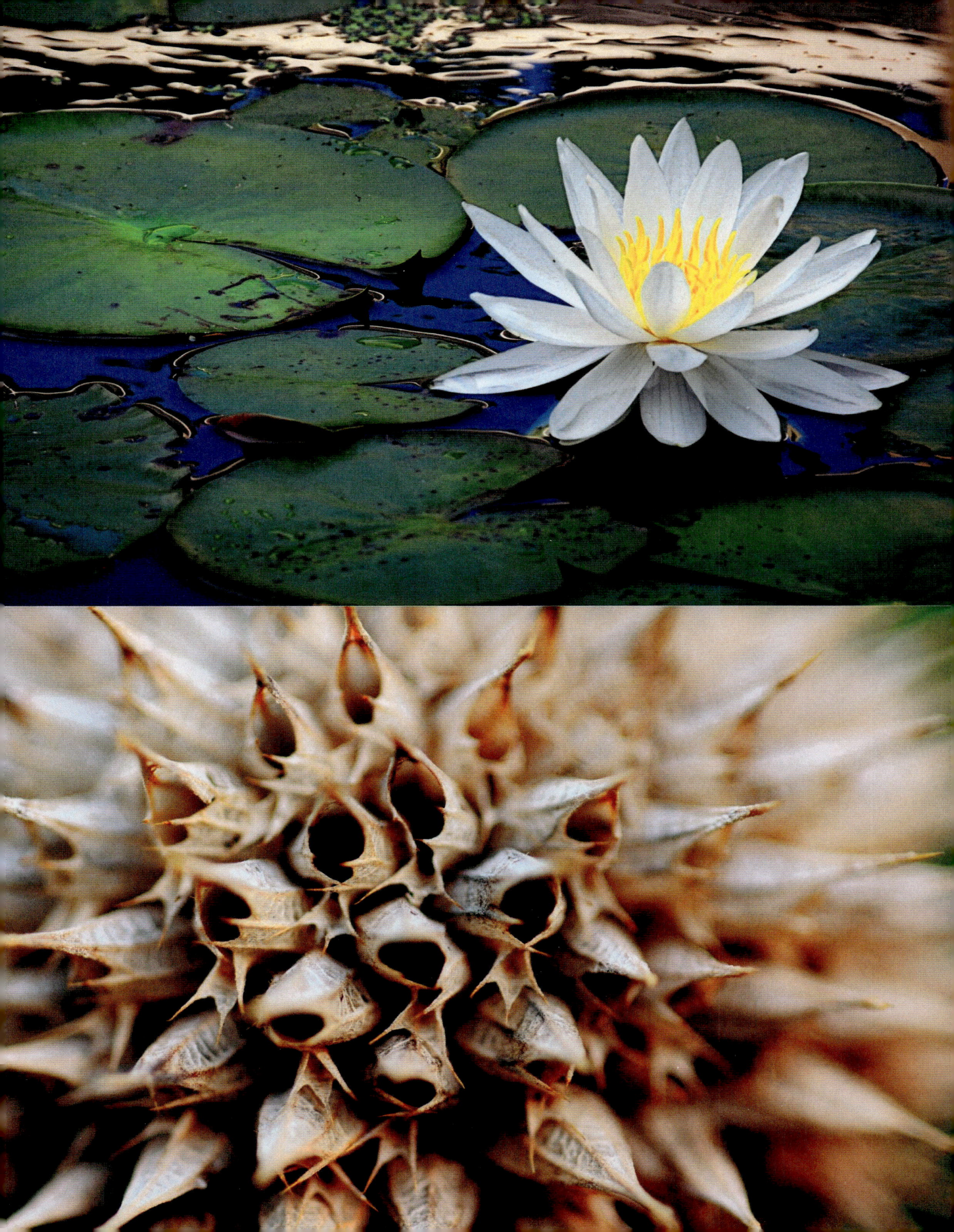

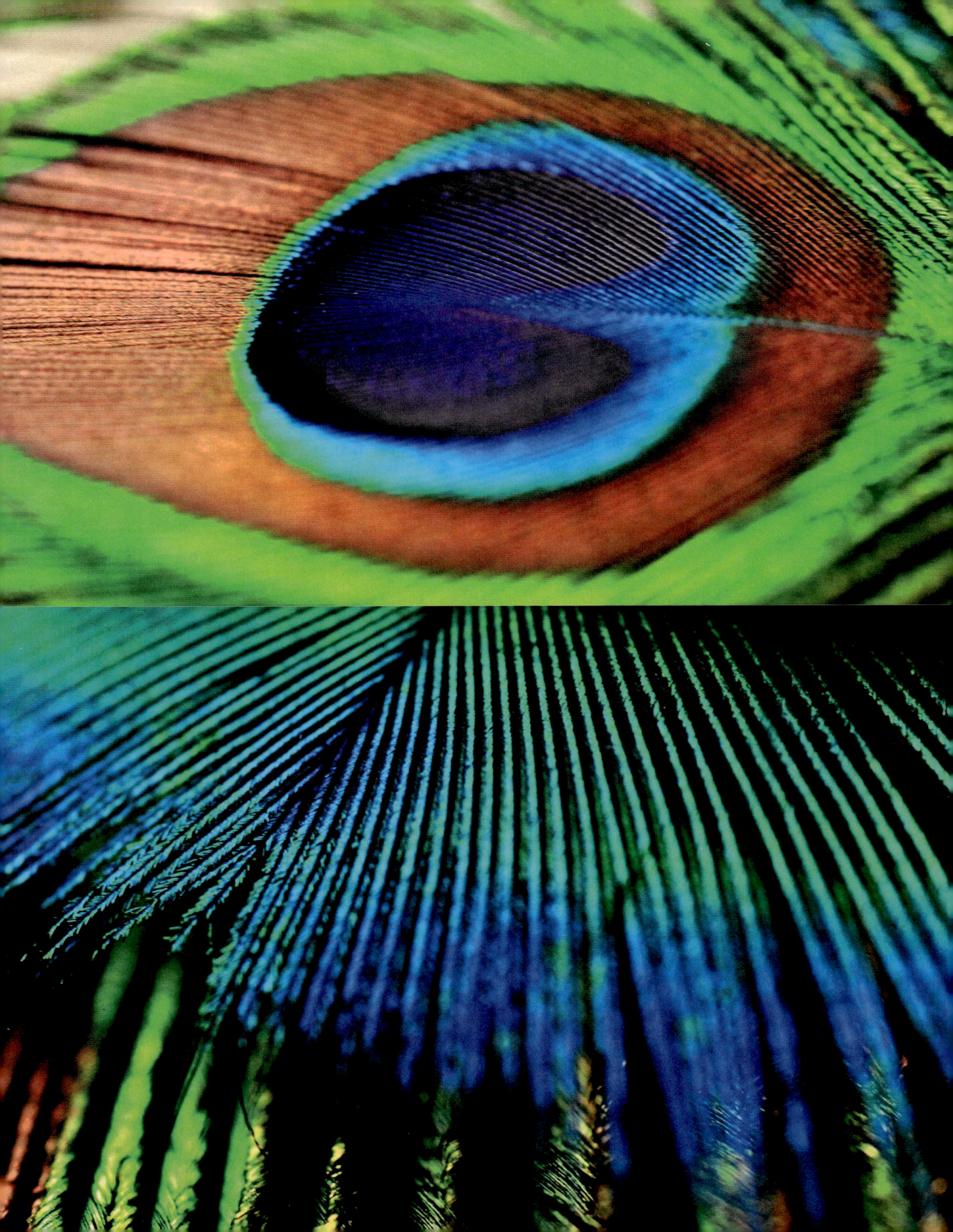

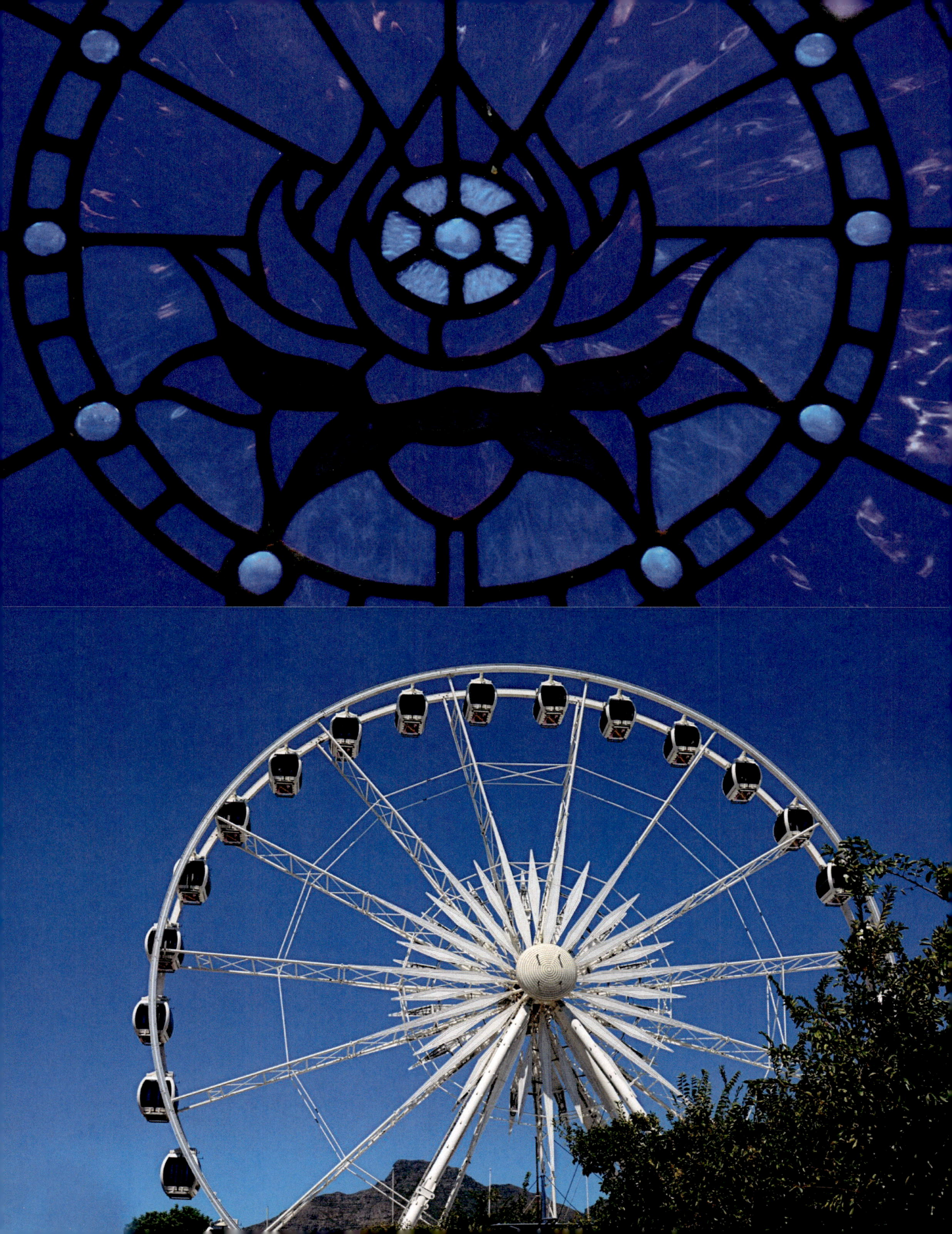

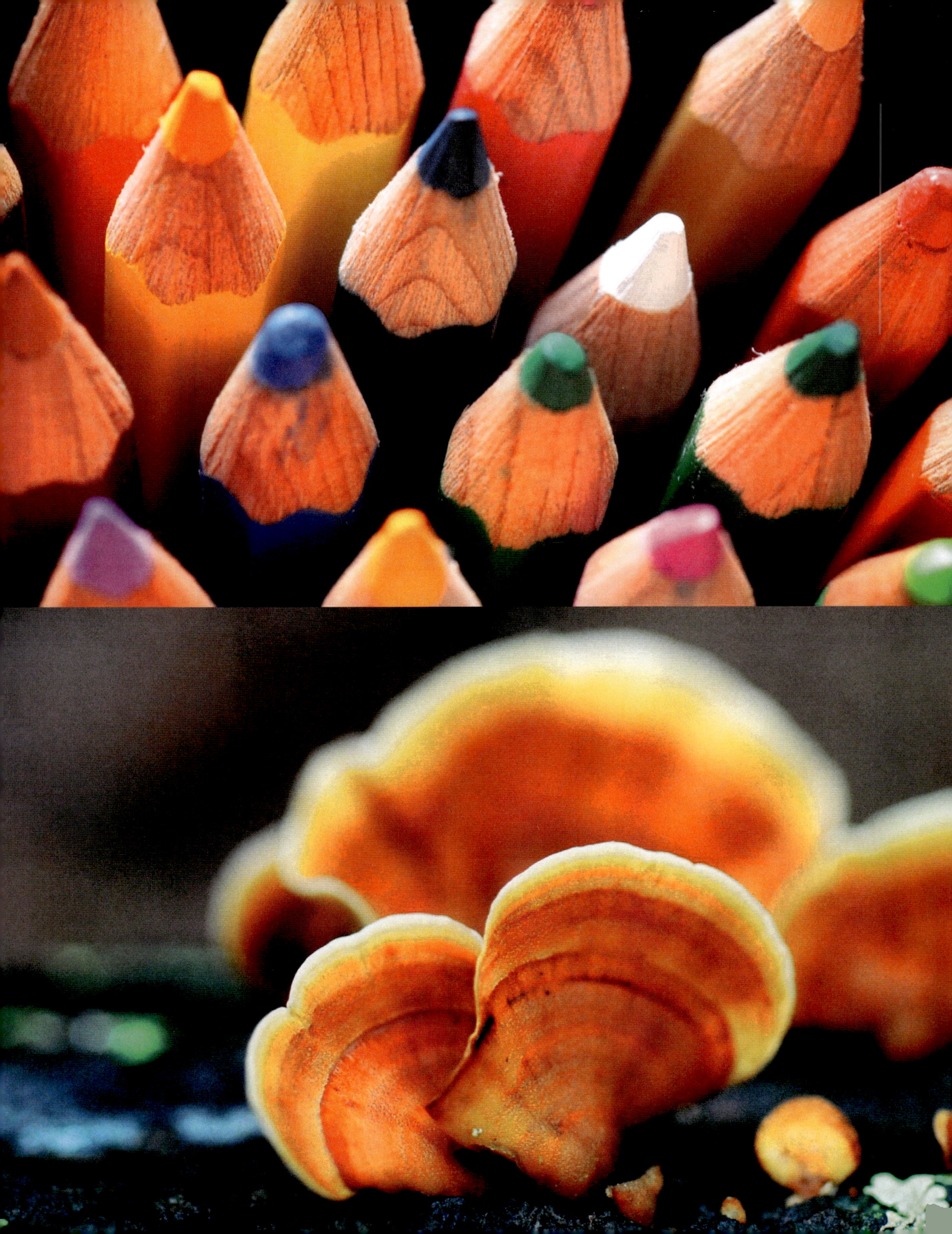

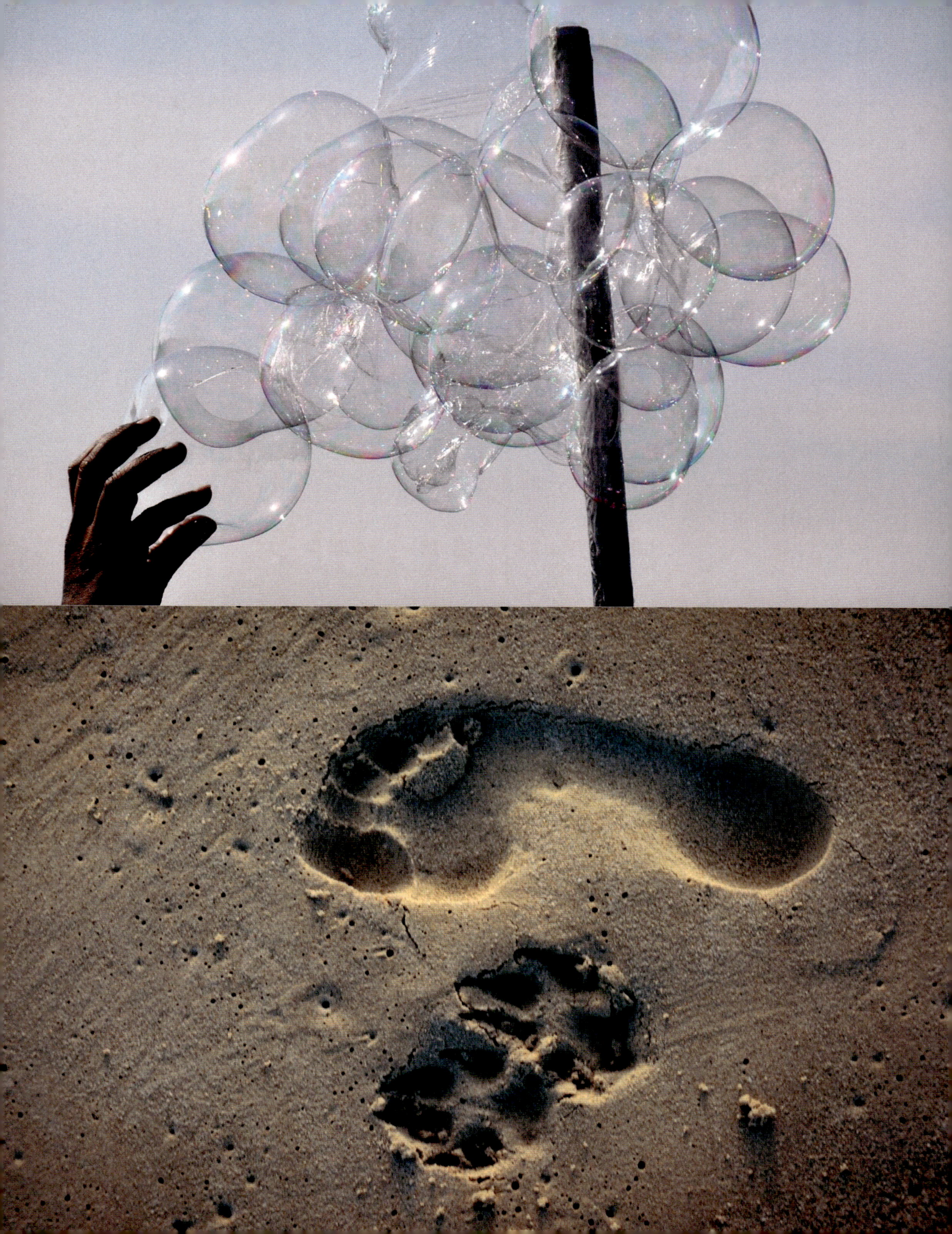

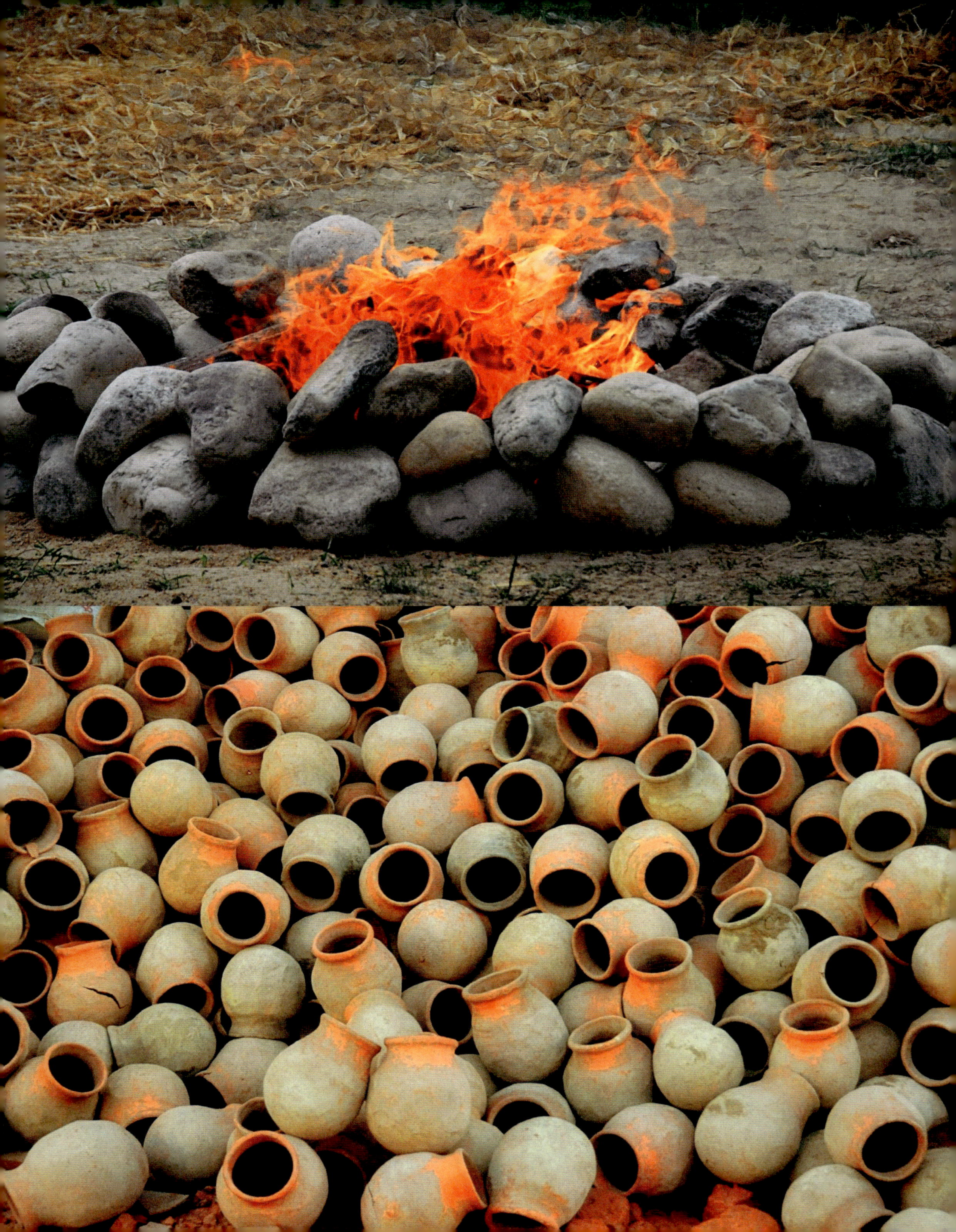

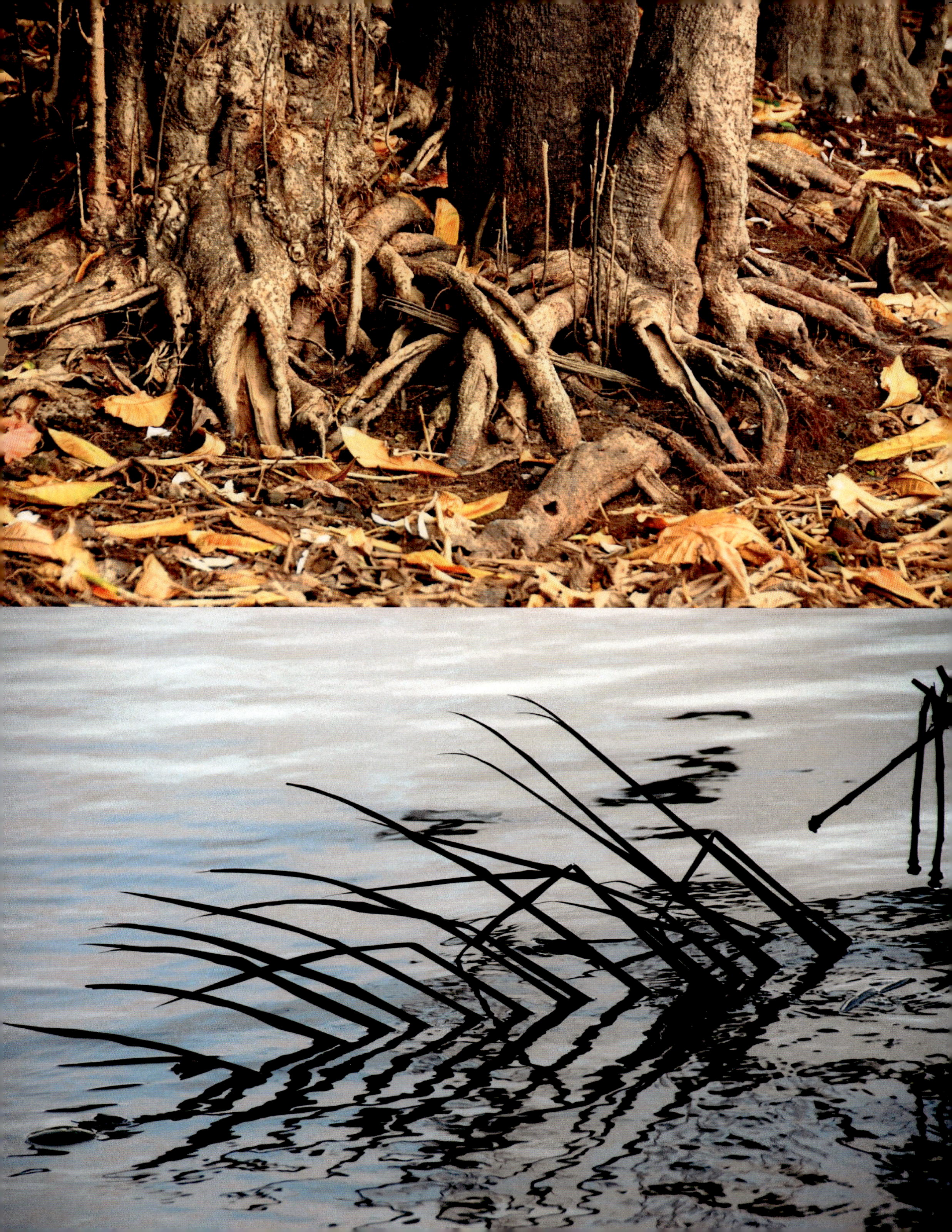

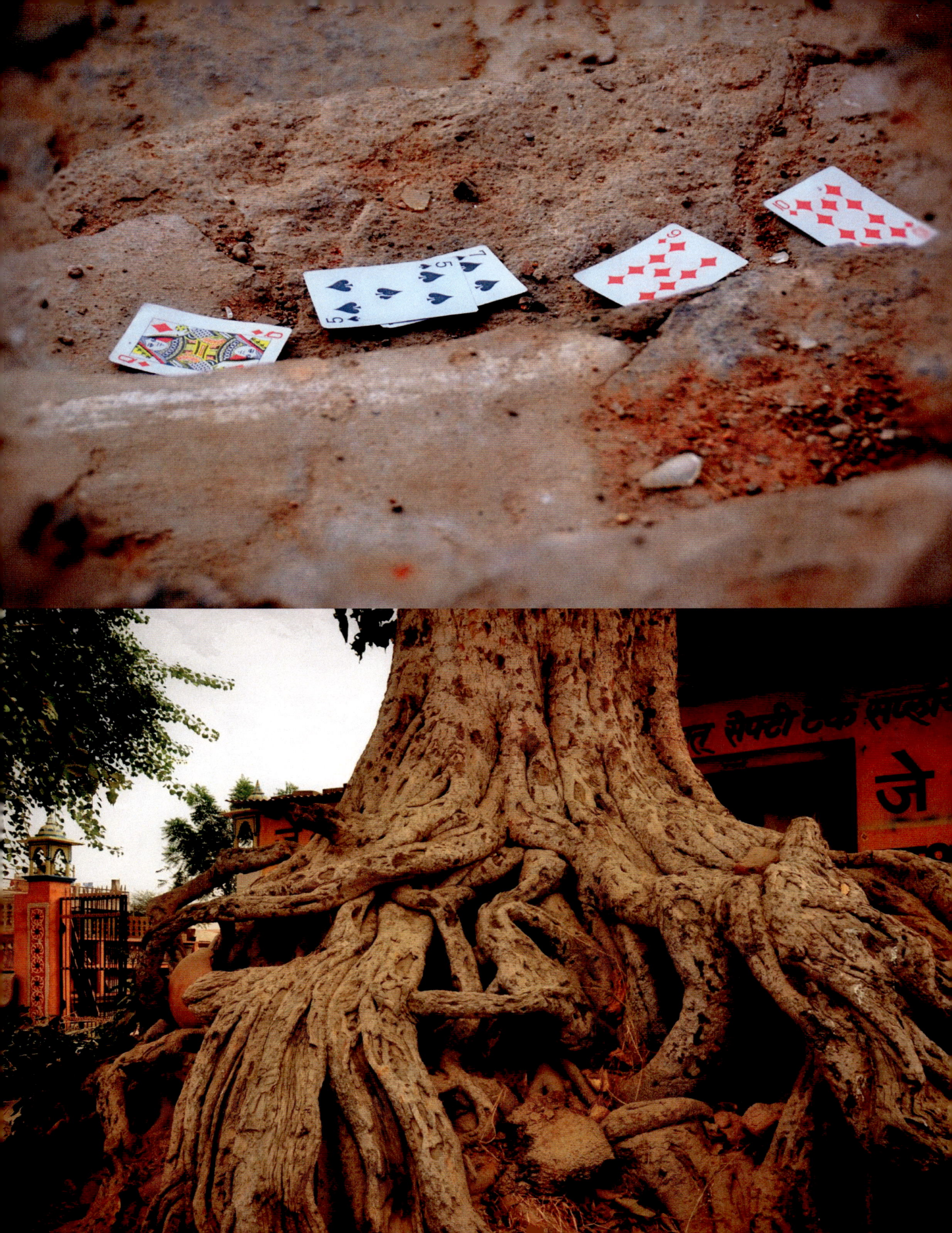

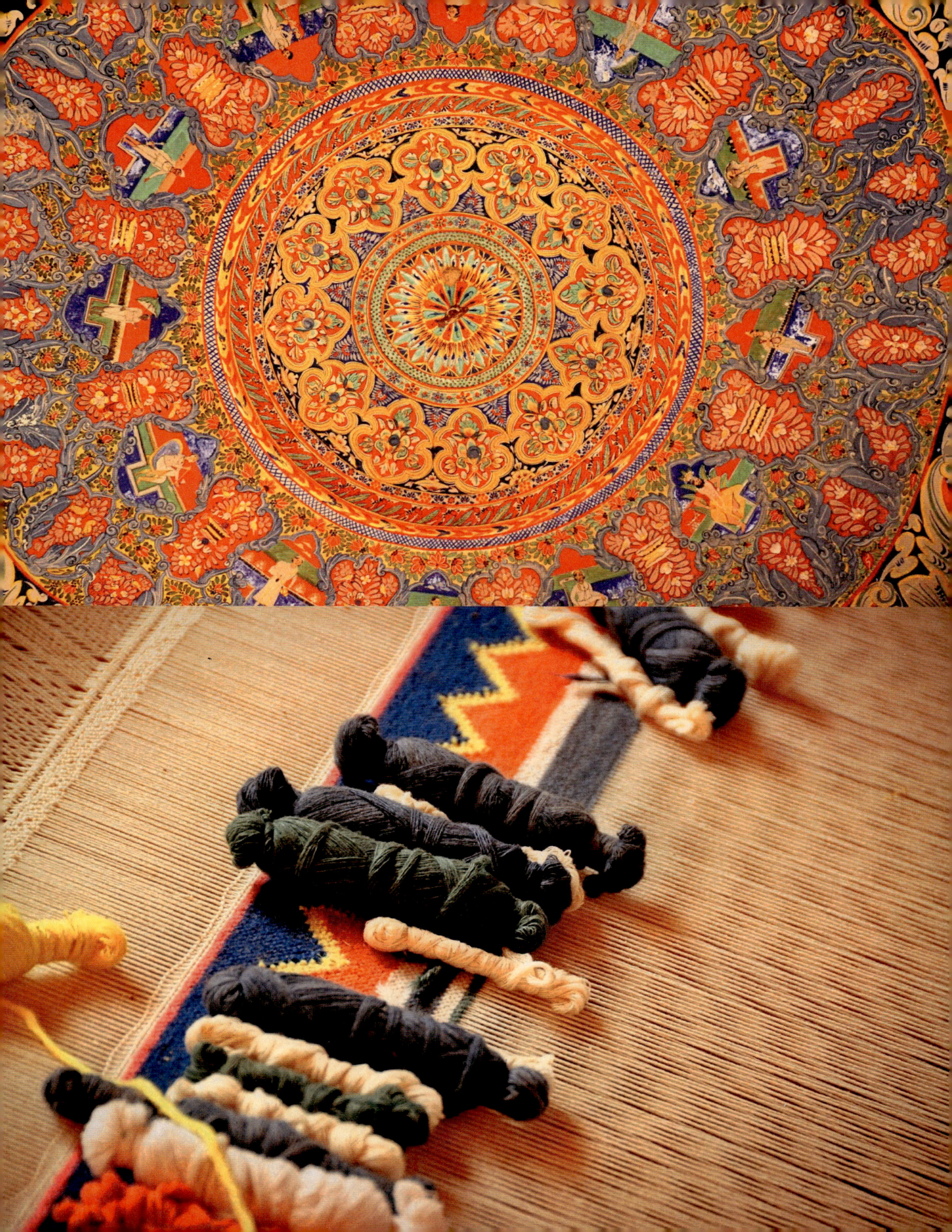

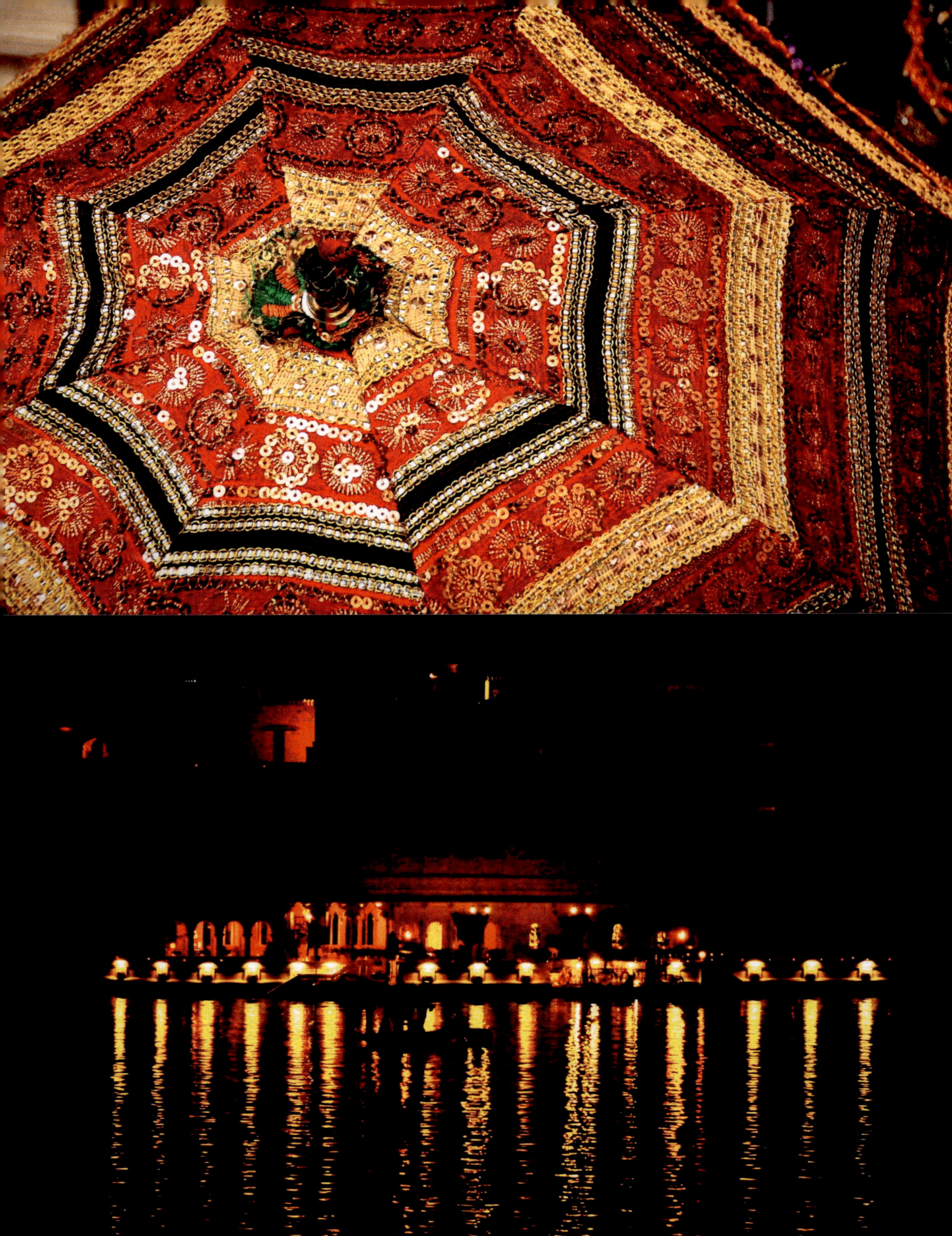

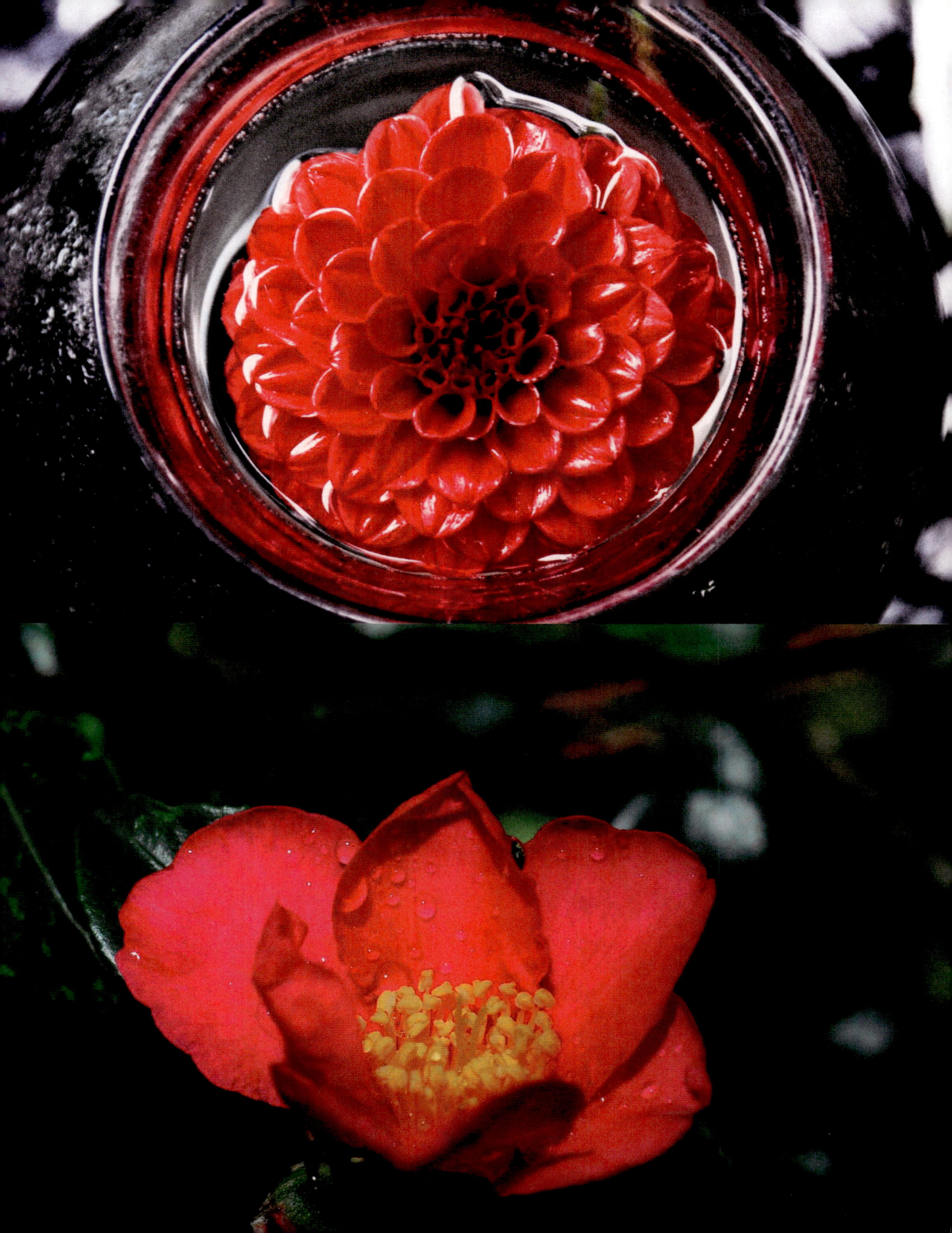

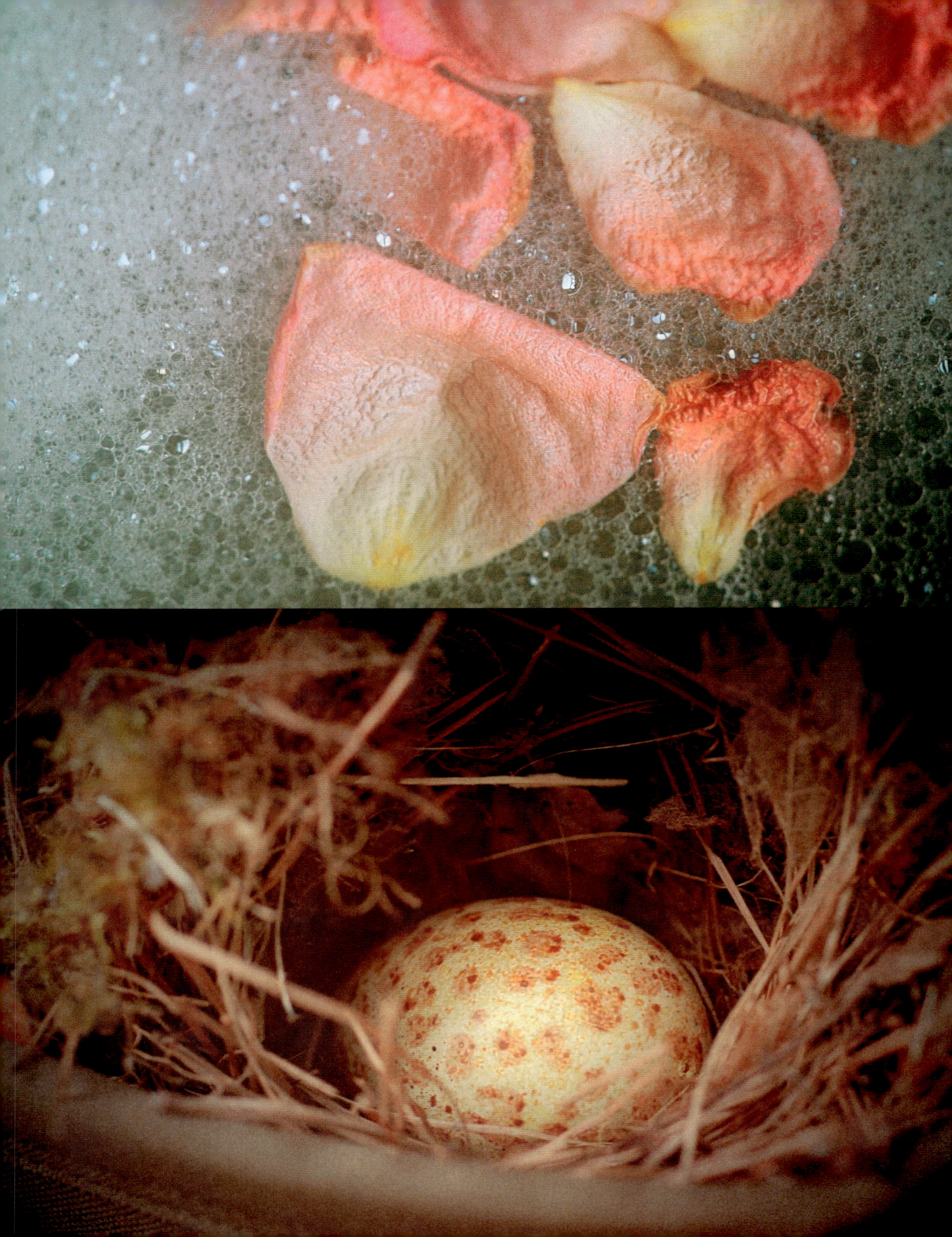

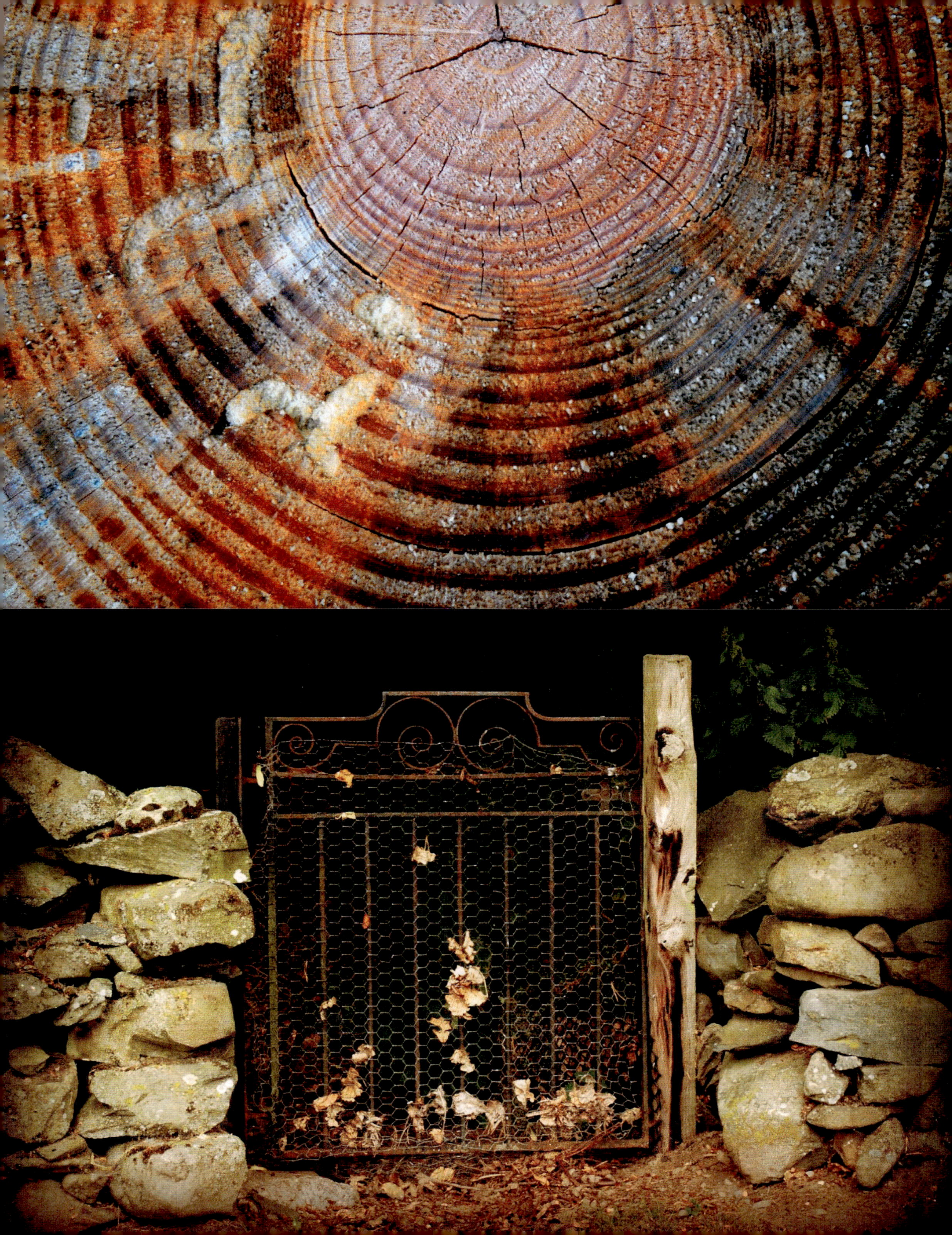

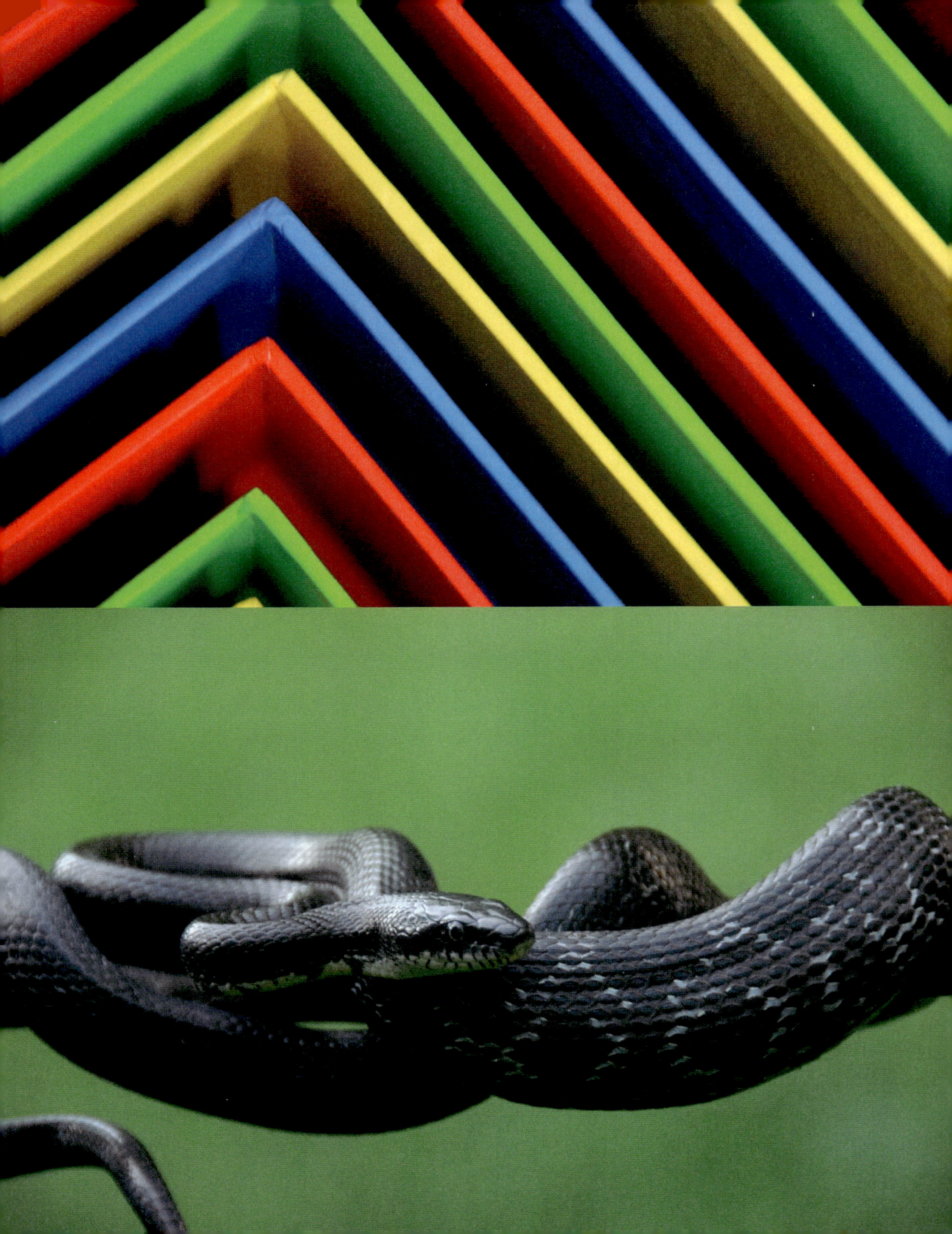

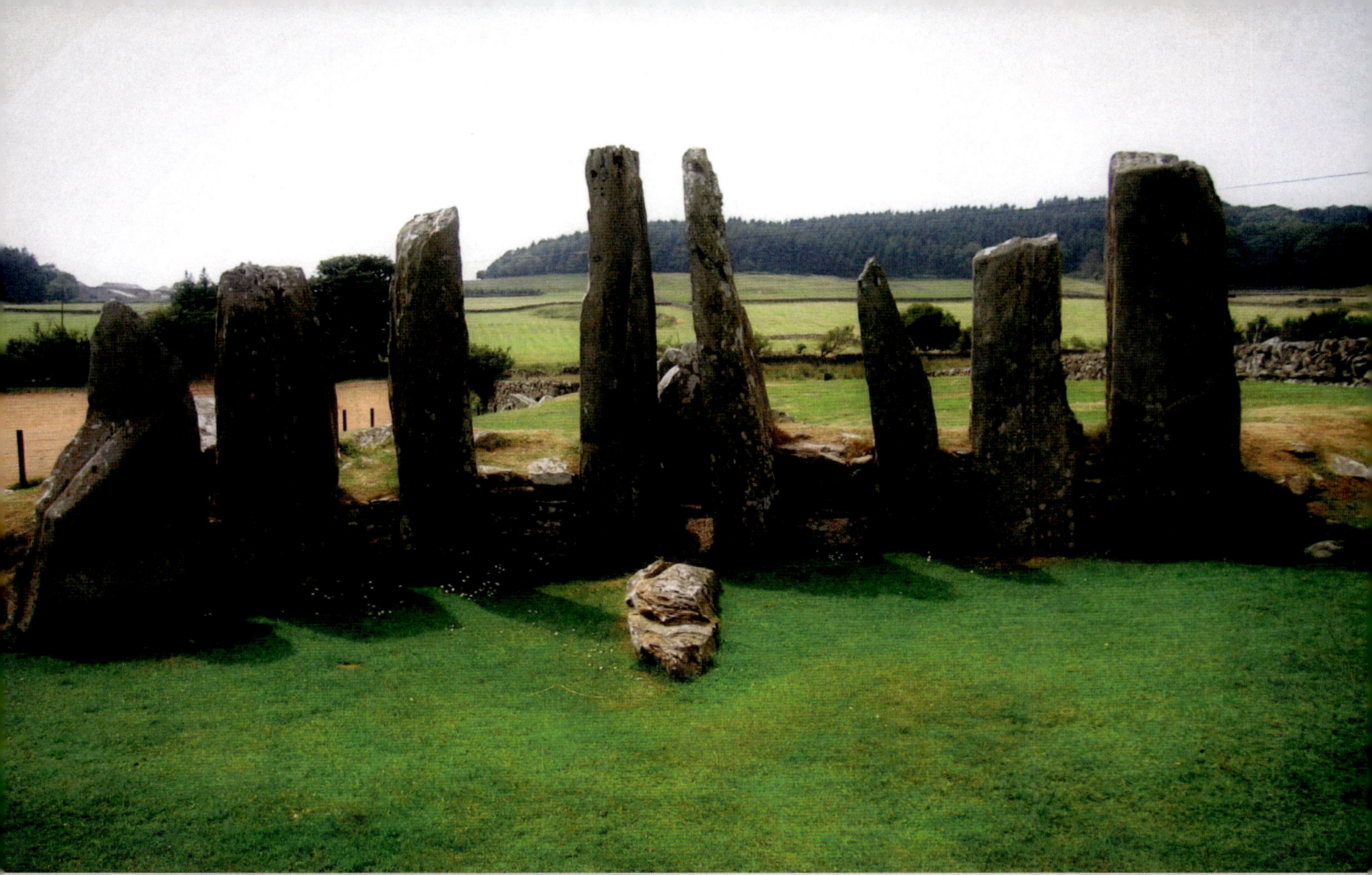

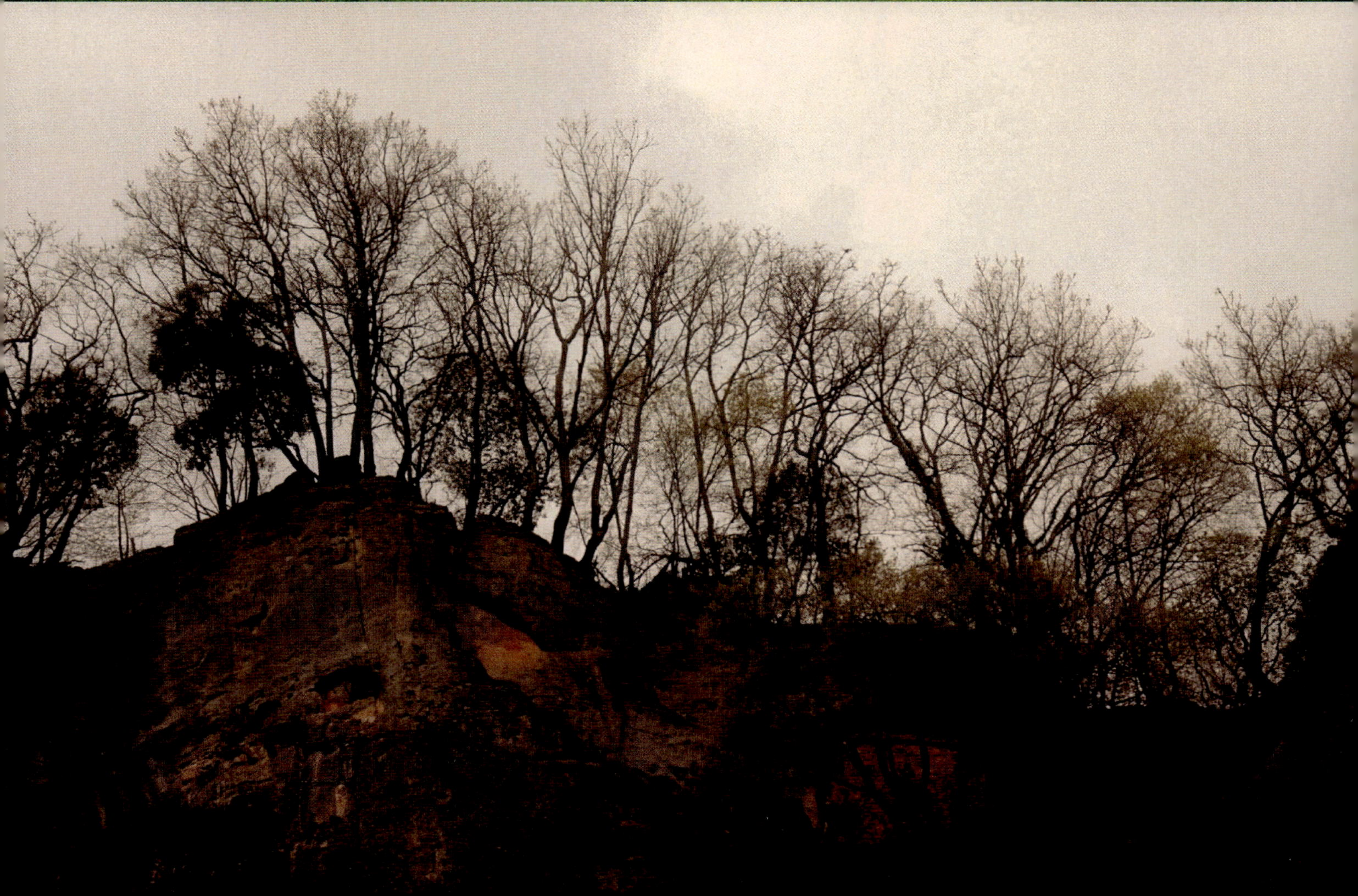

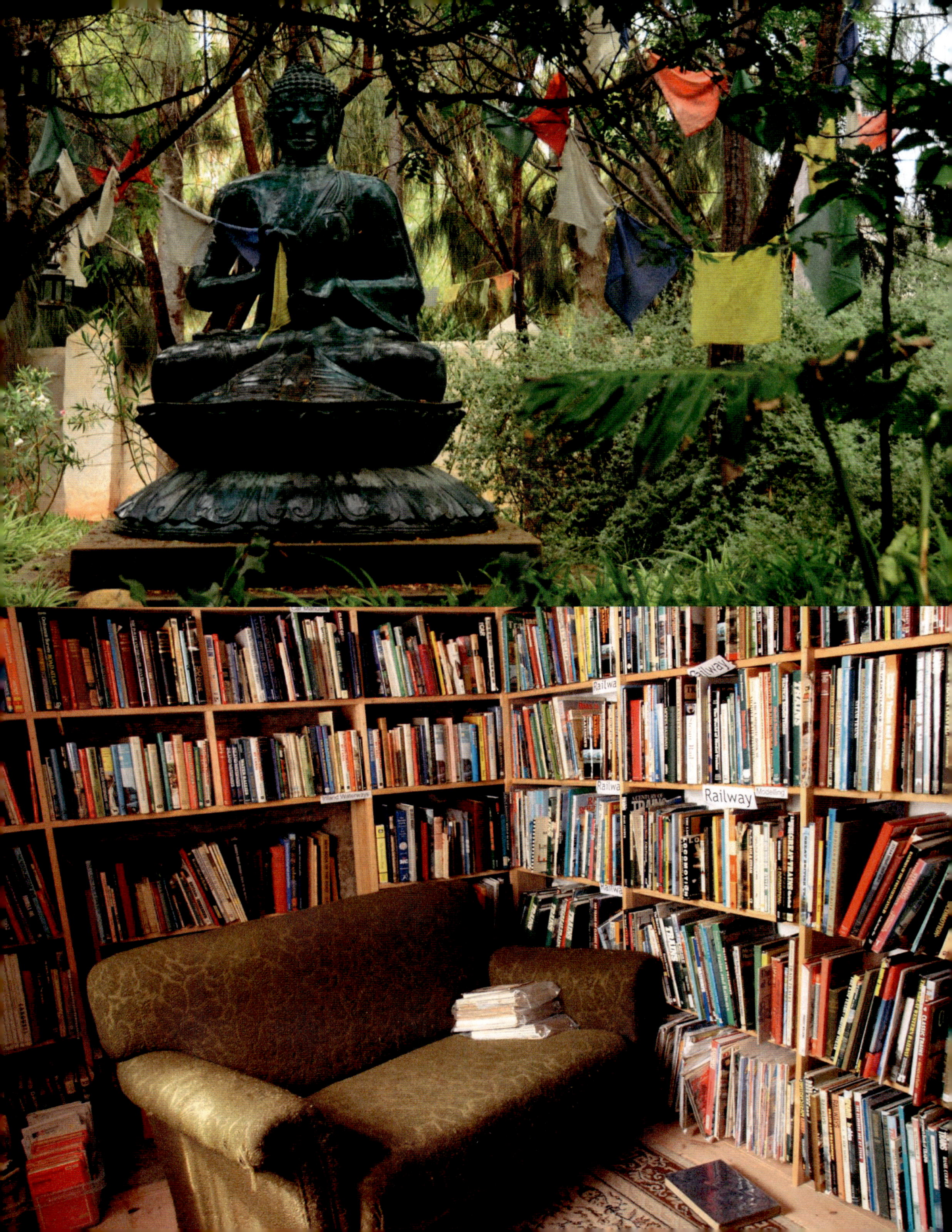
Railway
Railway
Modelling

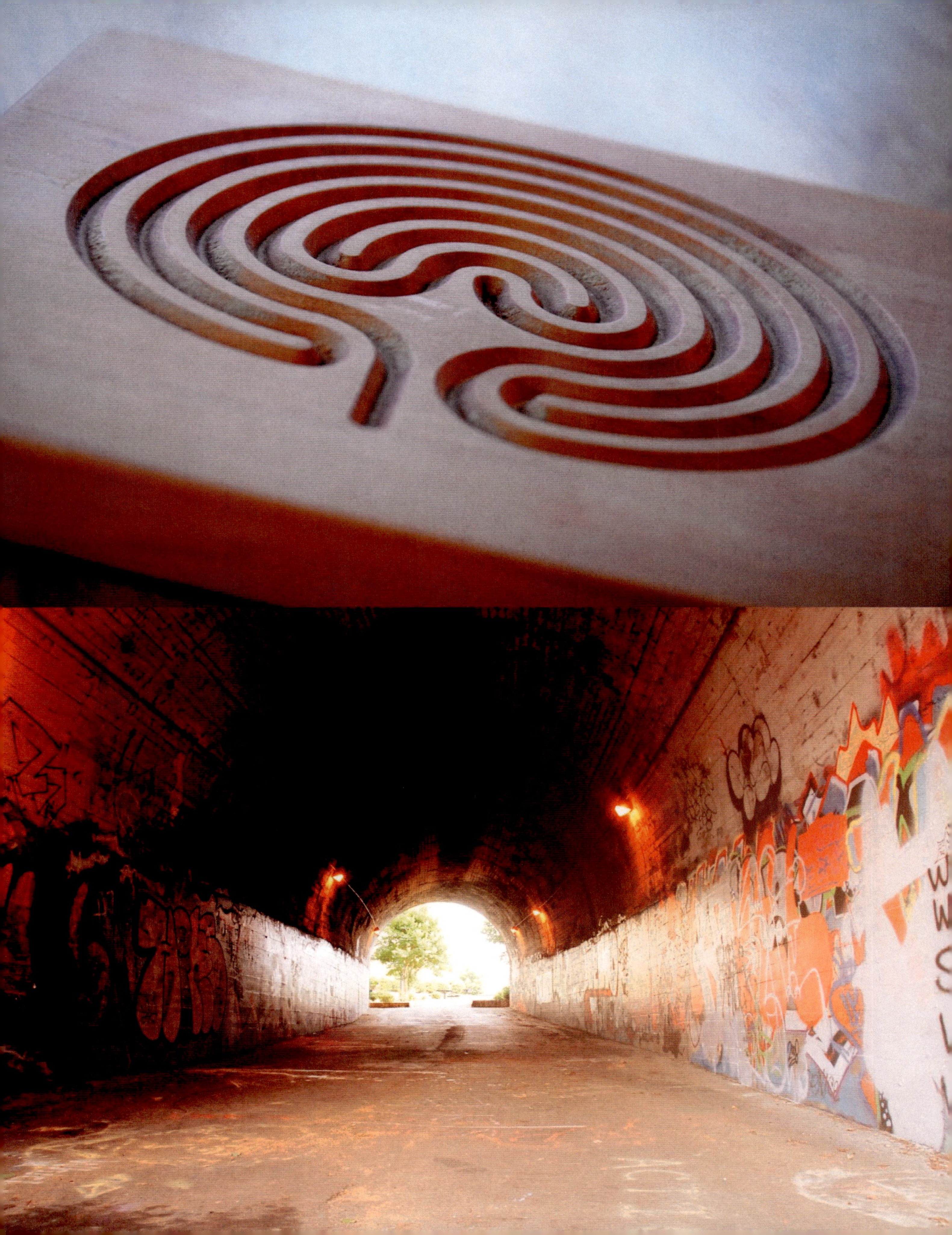

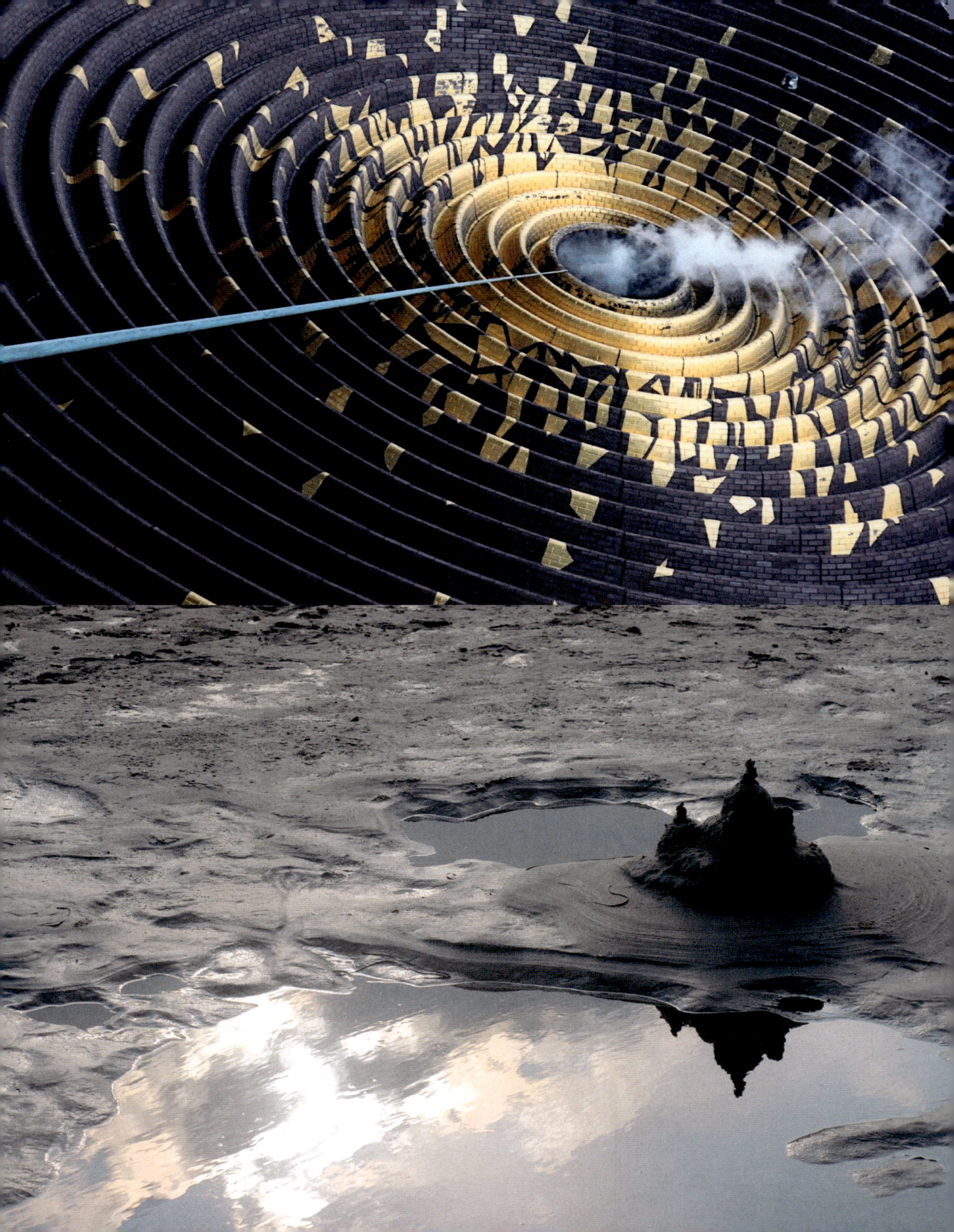

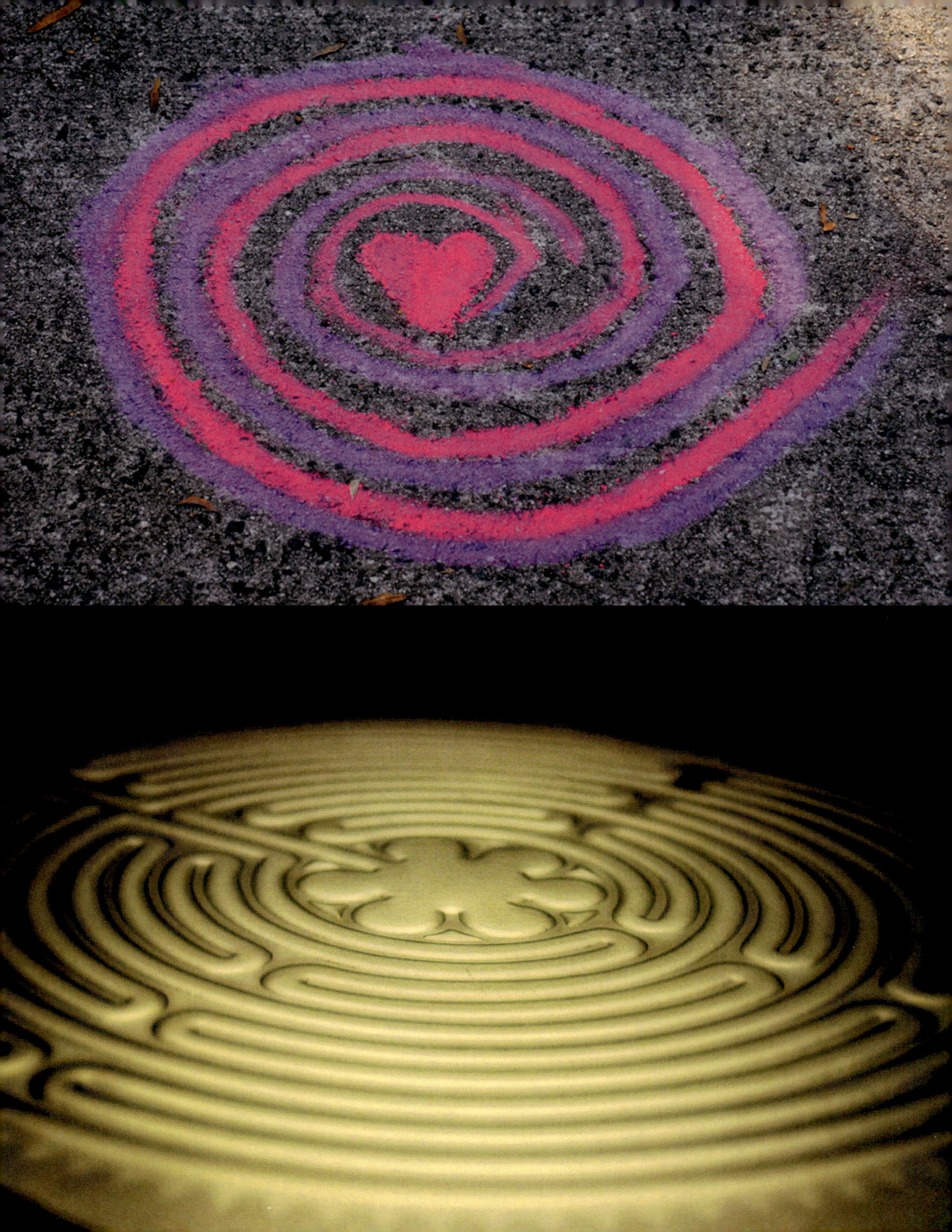

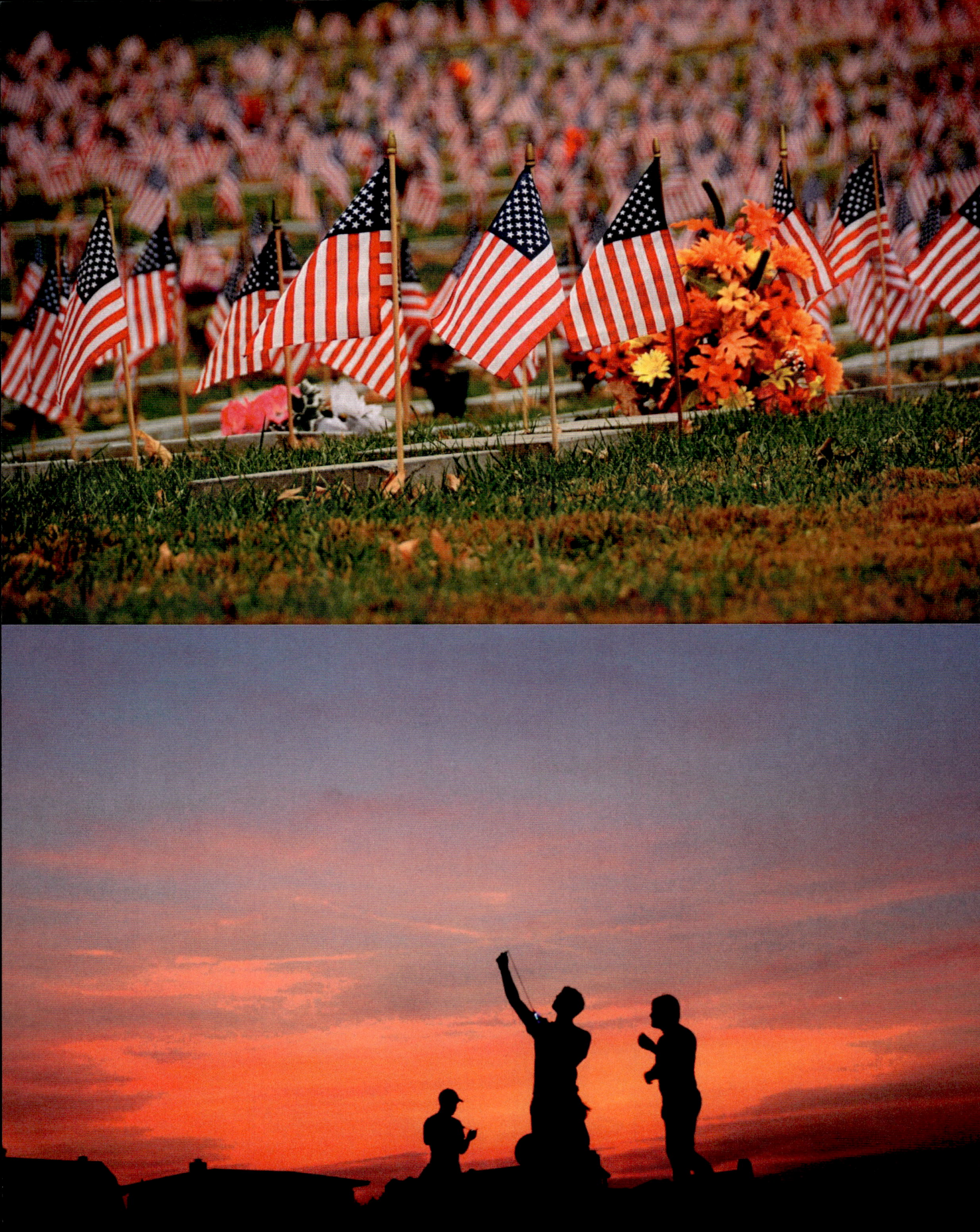

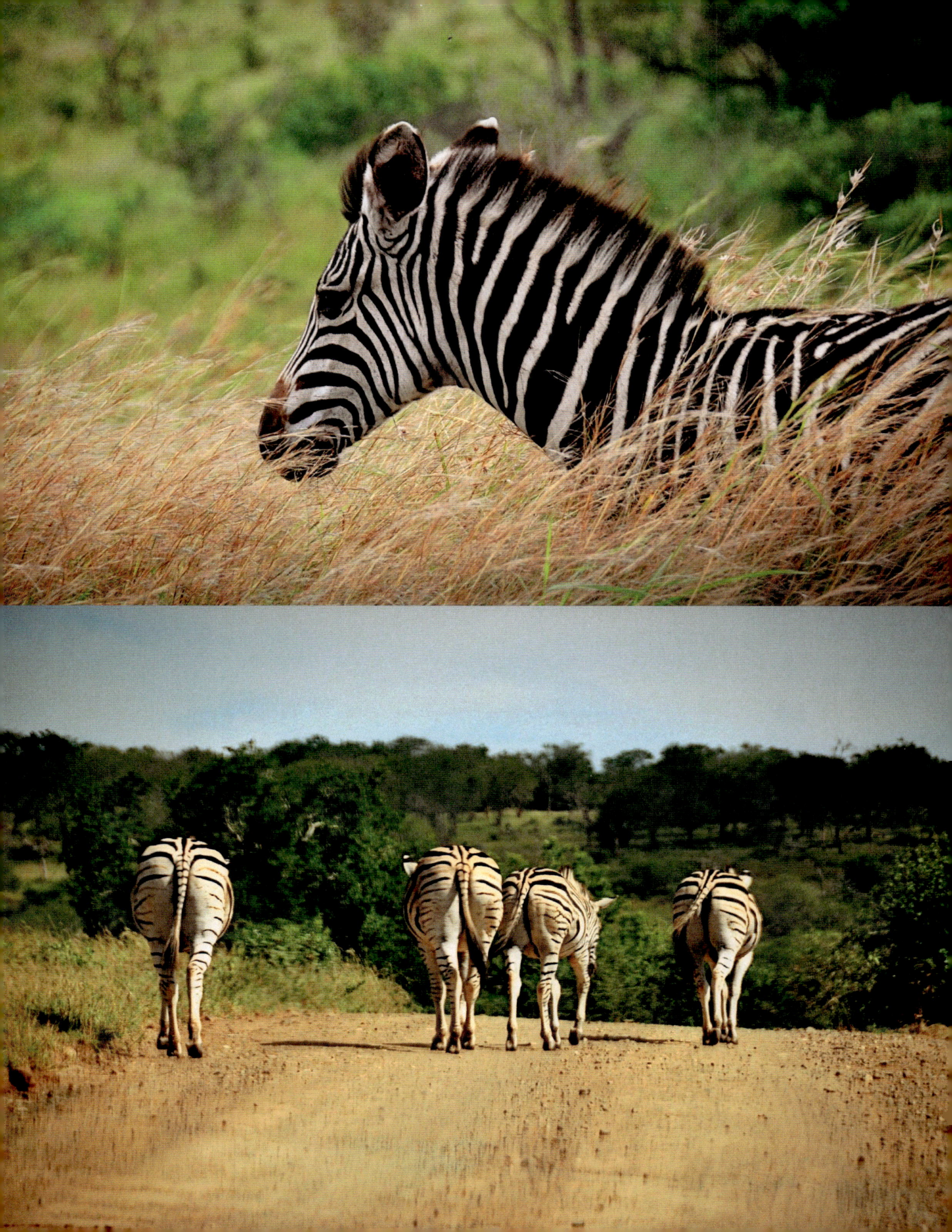

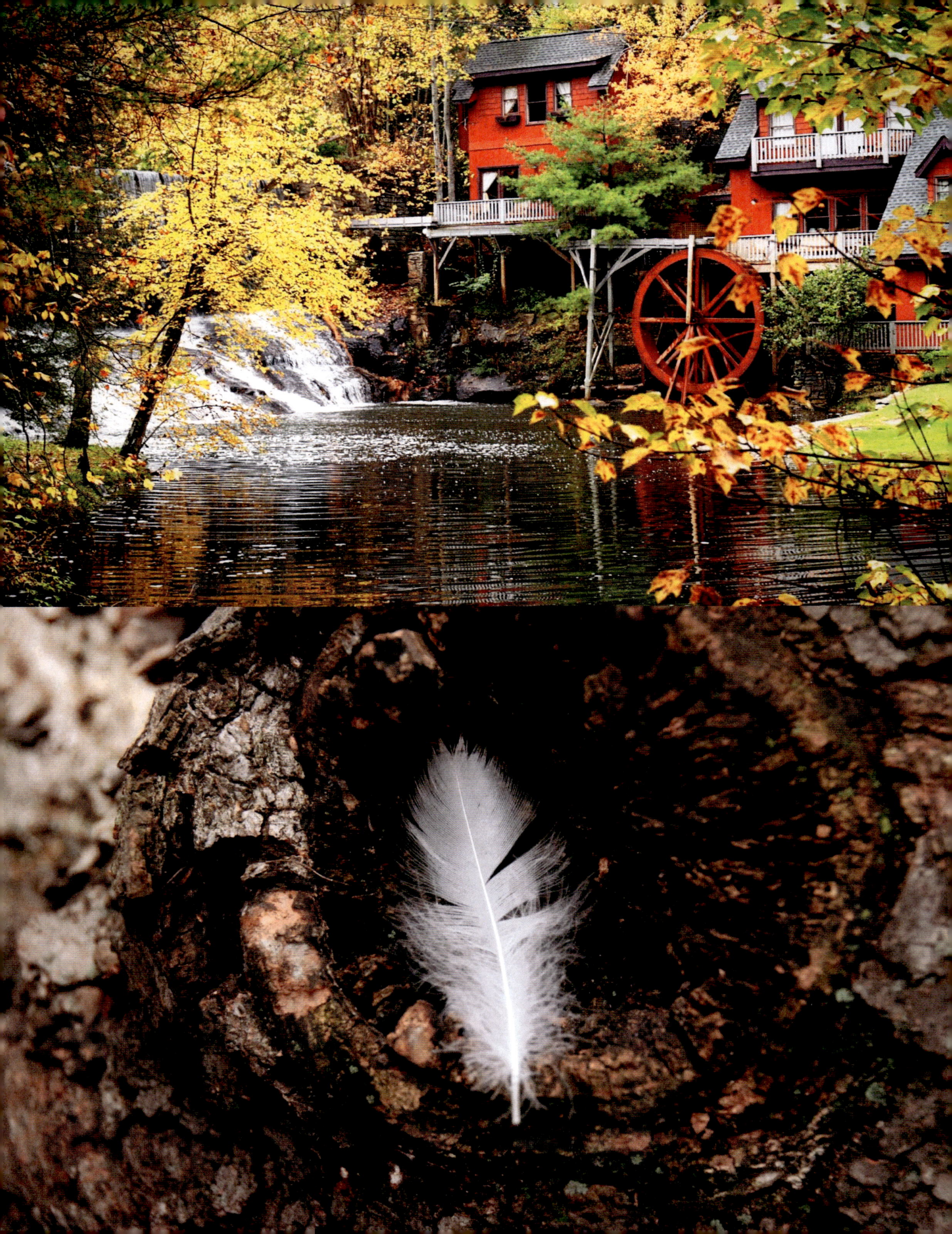

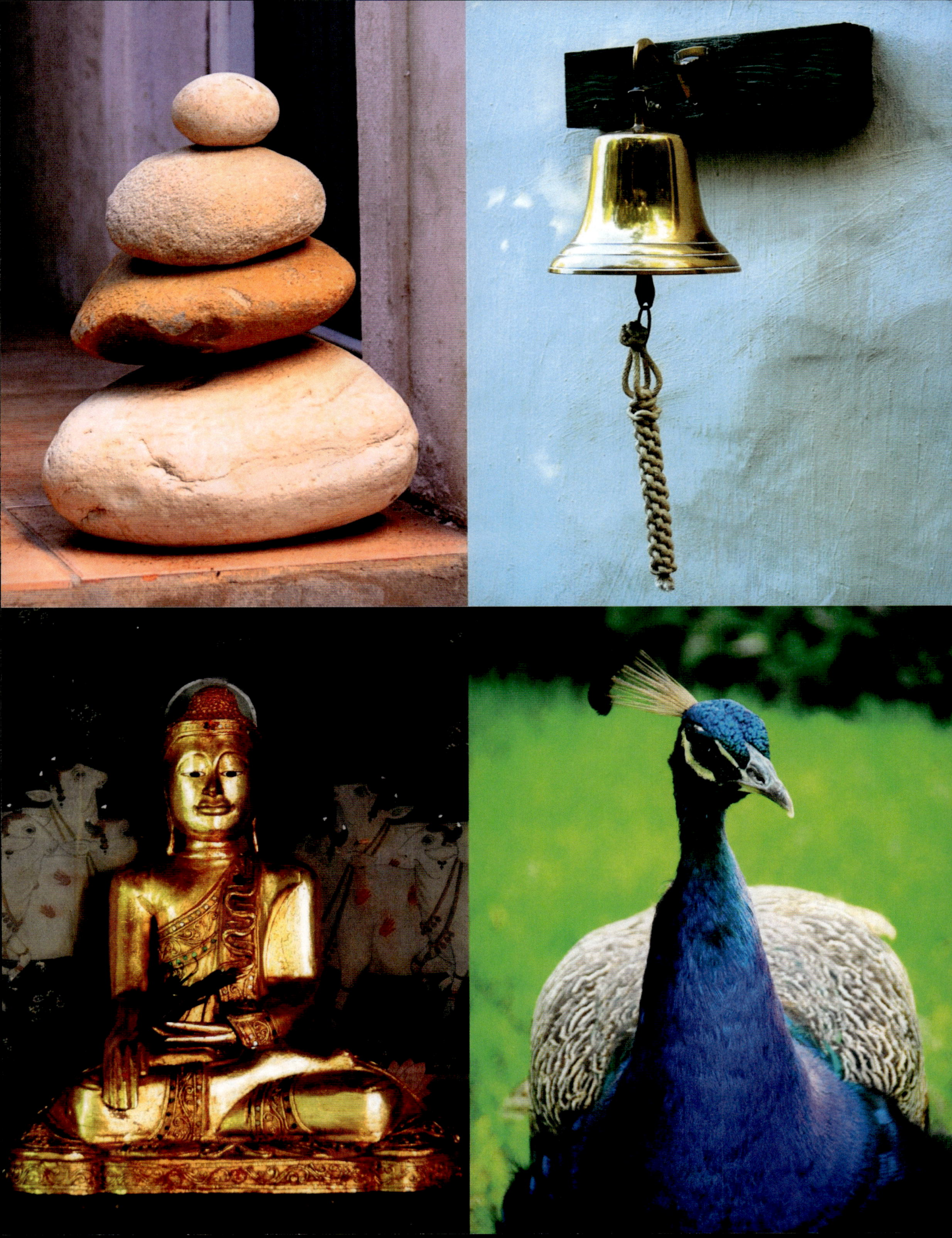

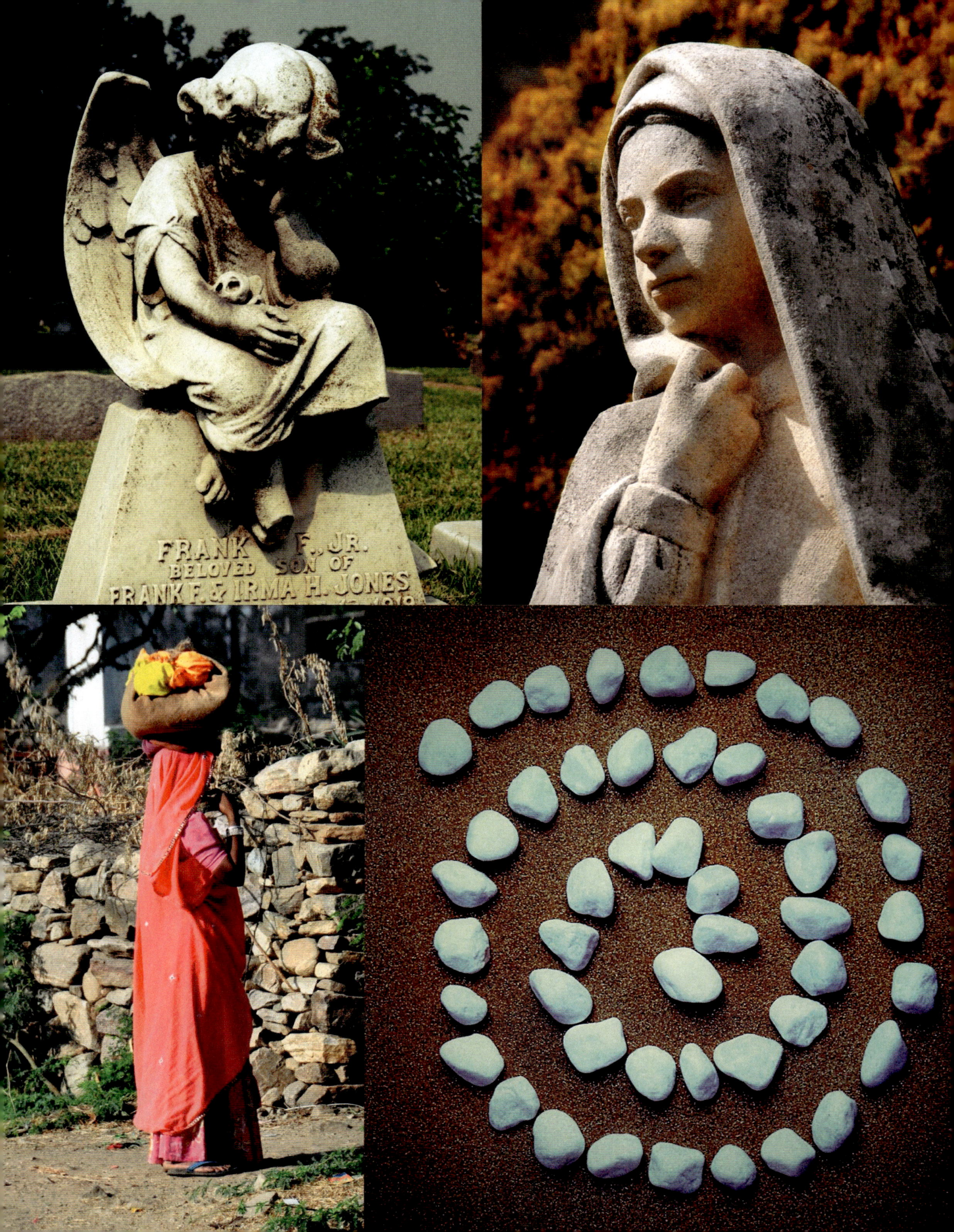
FRANK F., JR.
BELOVED SON OF
FRANK F. & IRMA H. JONES

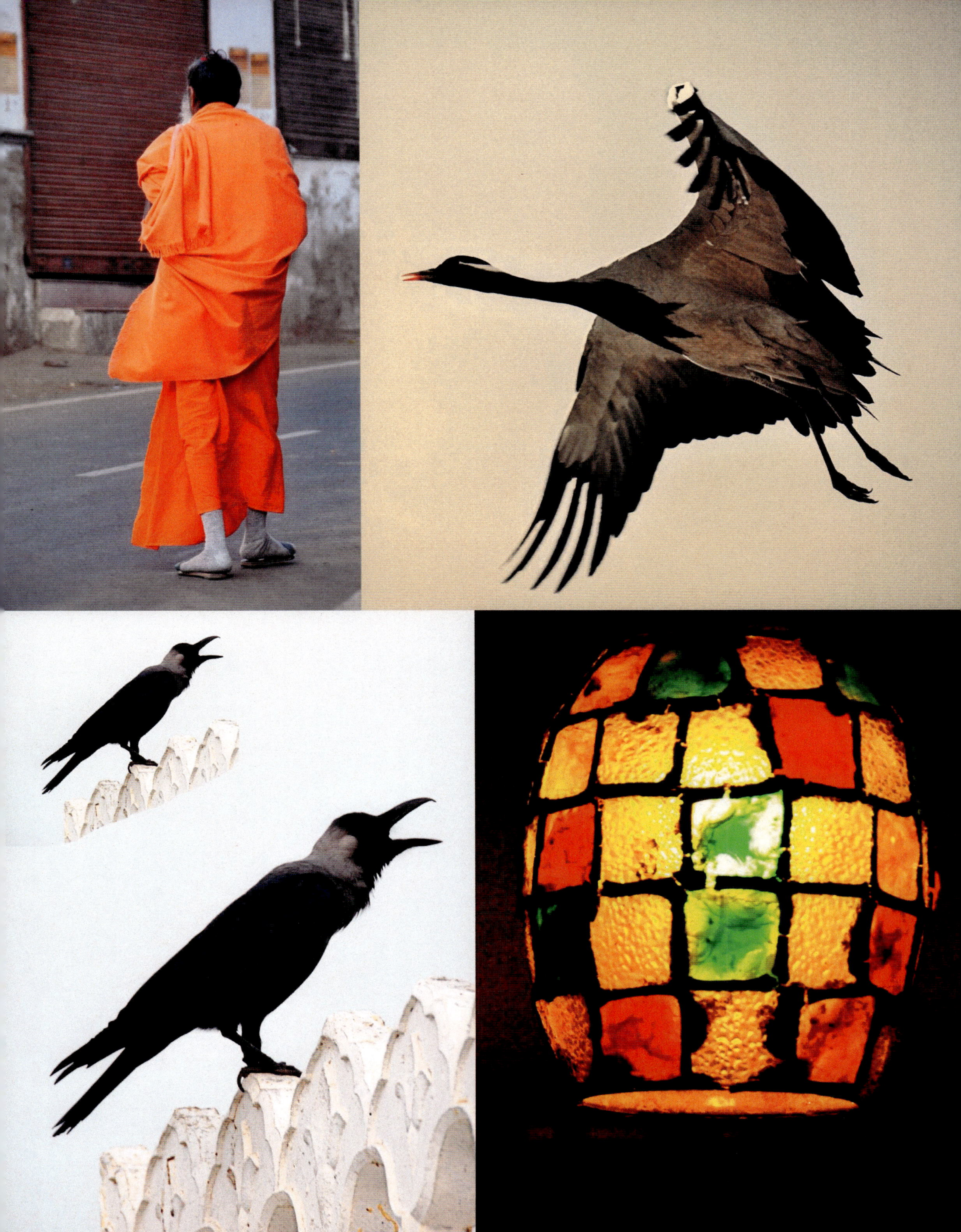

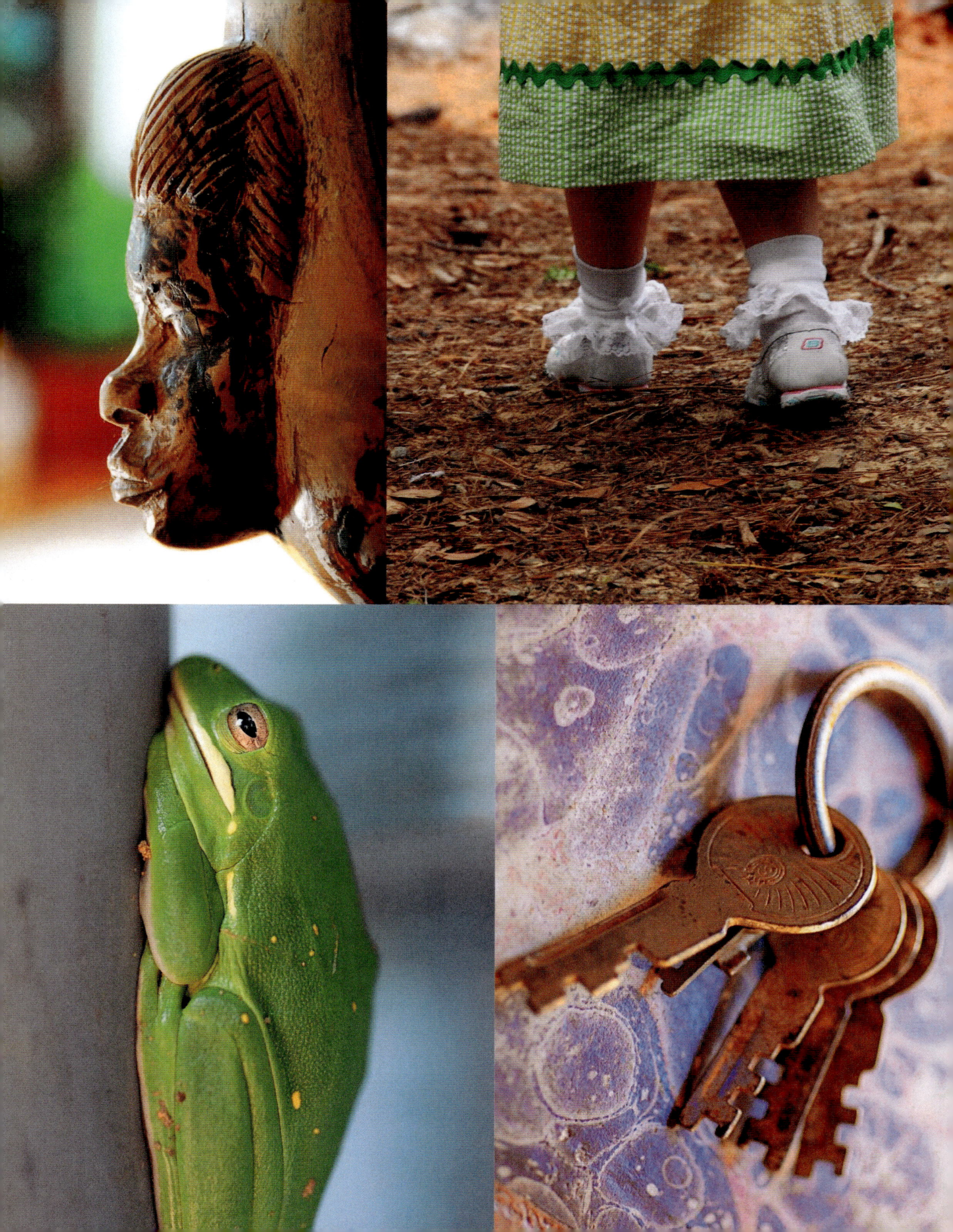

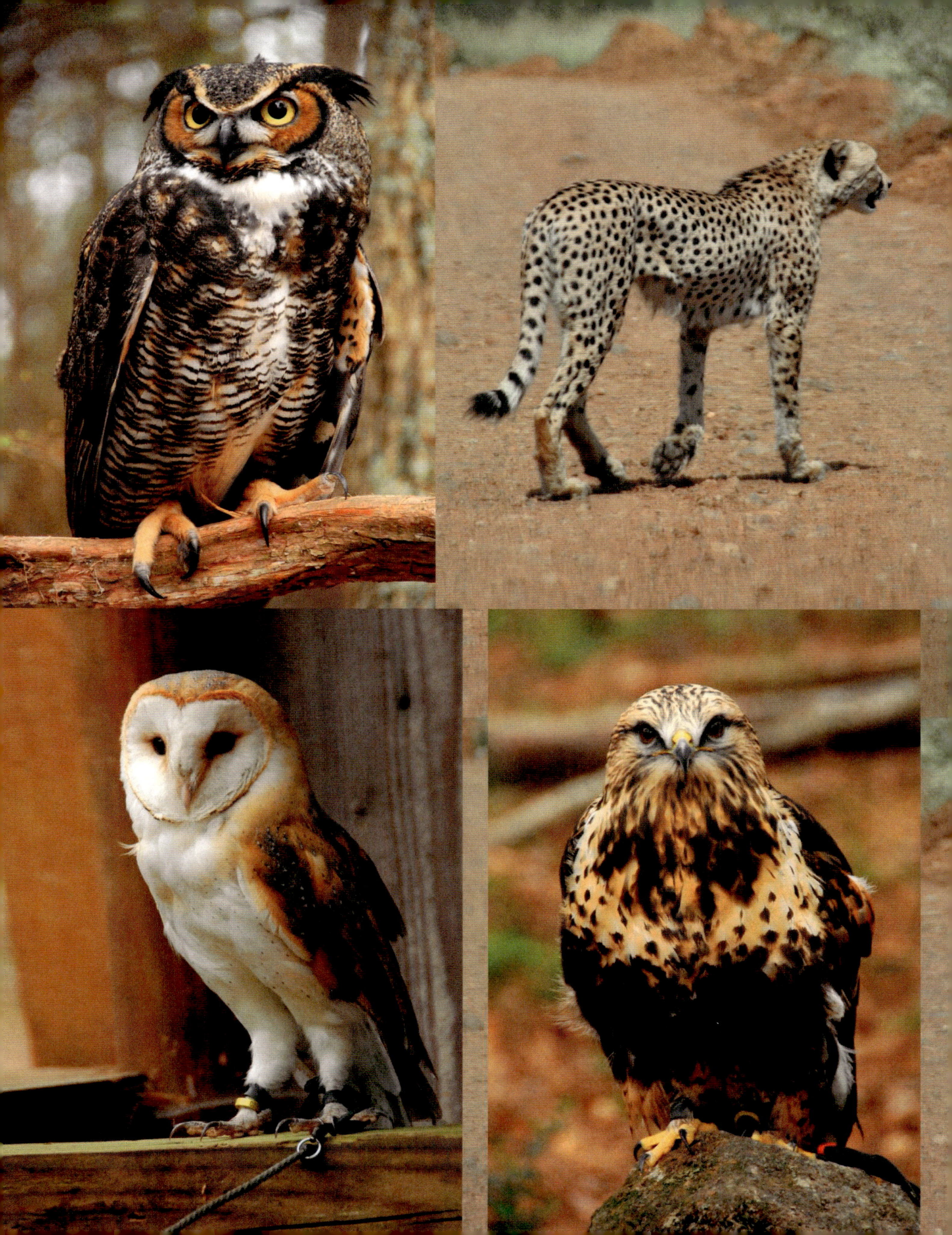

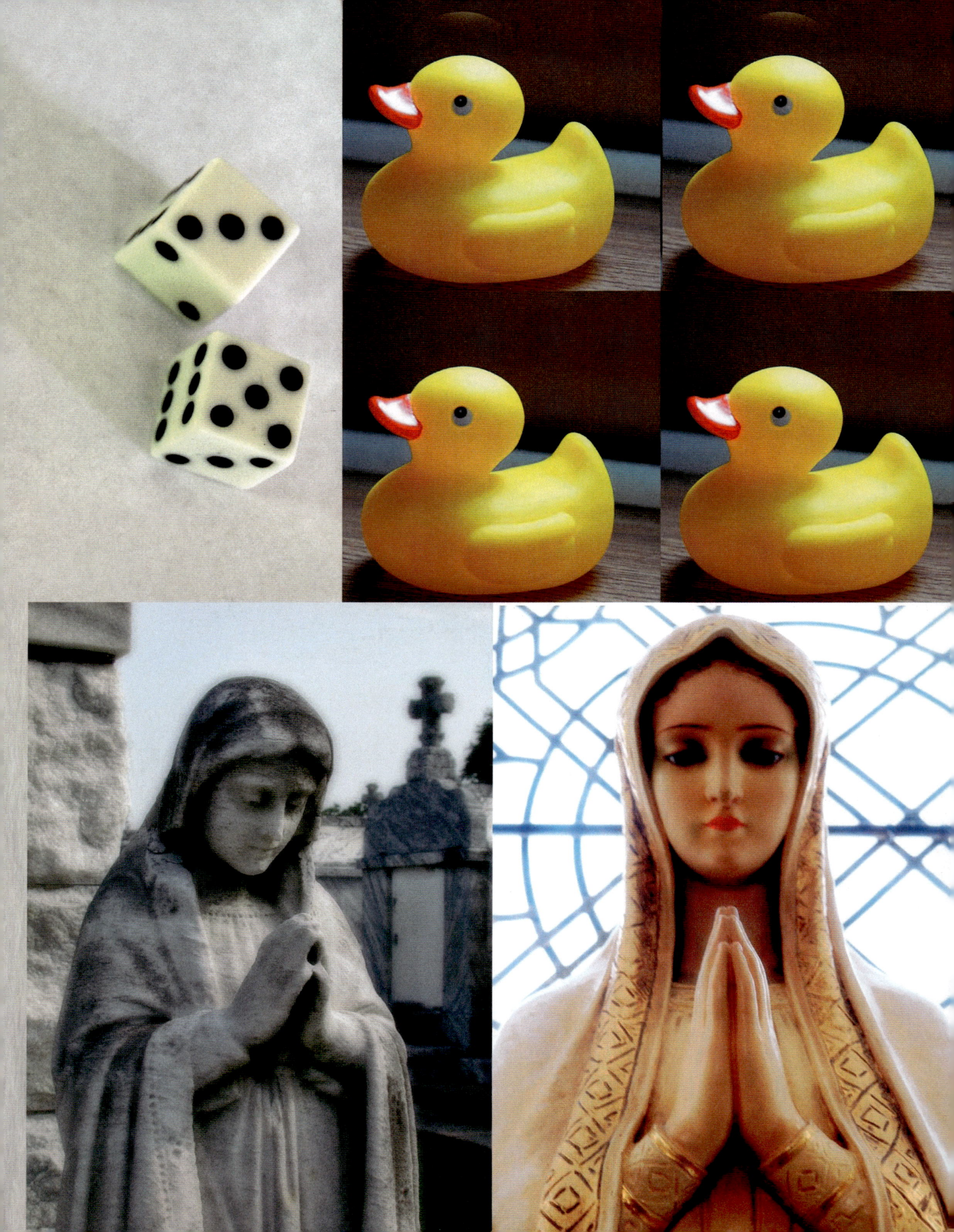

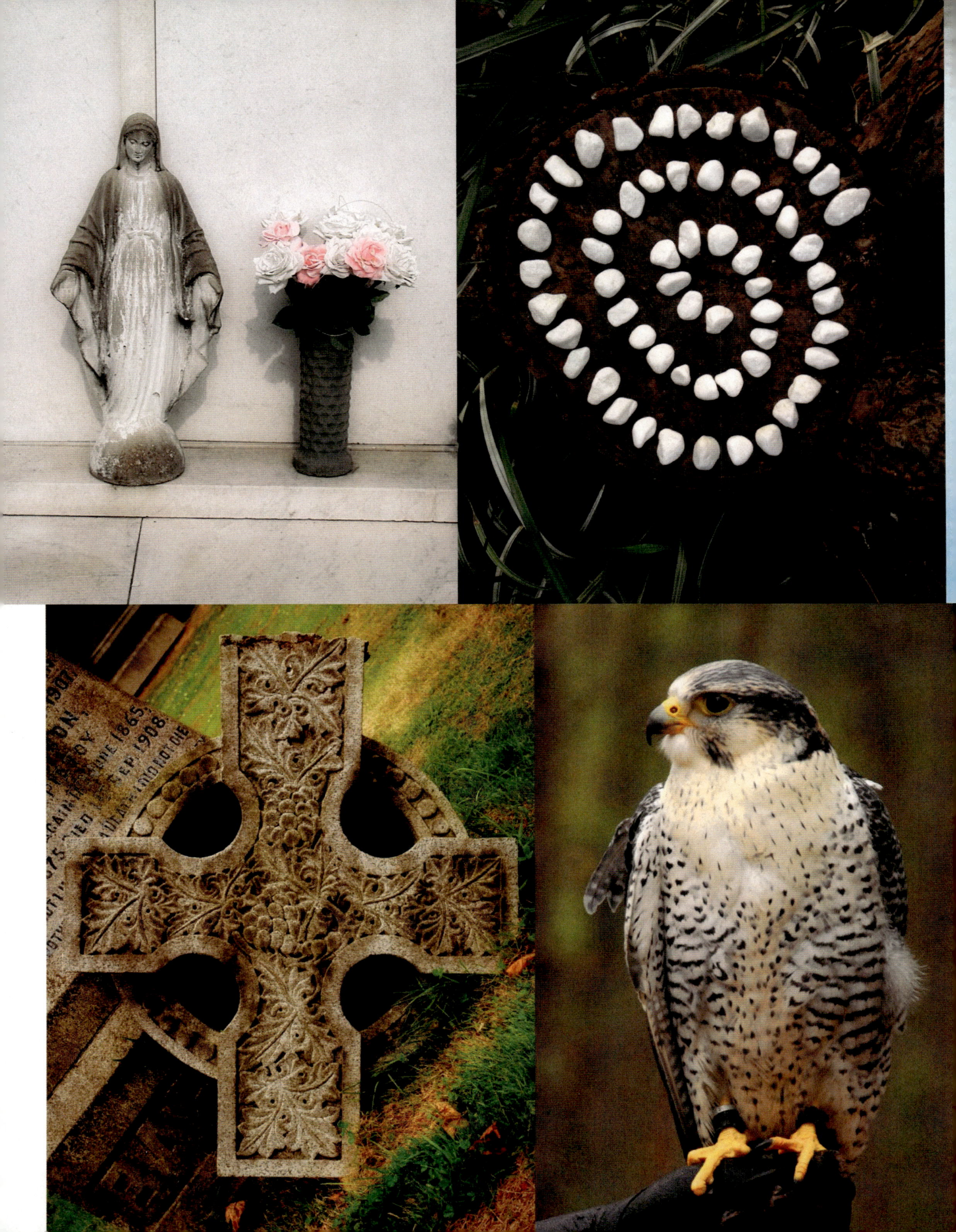

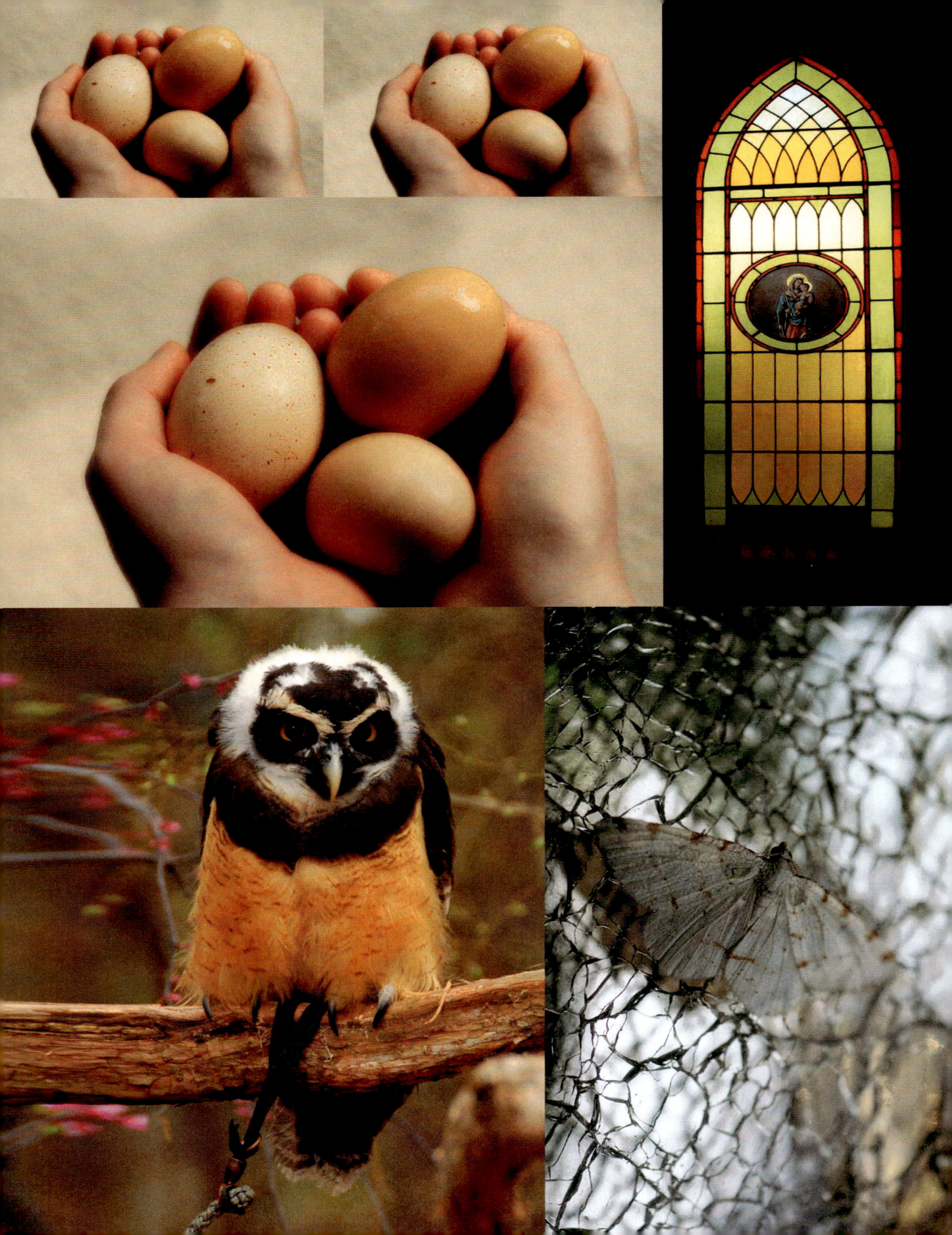

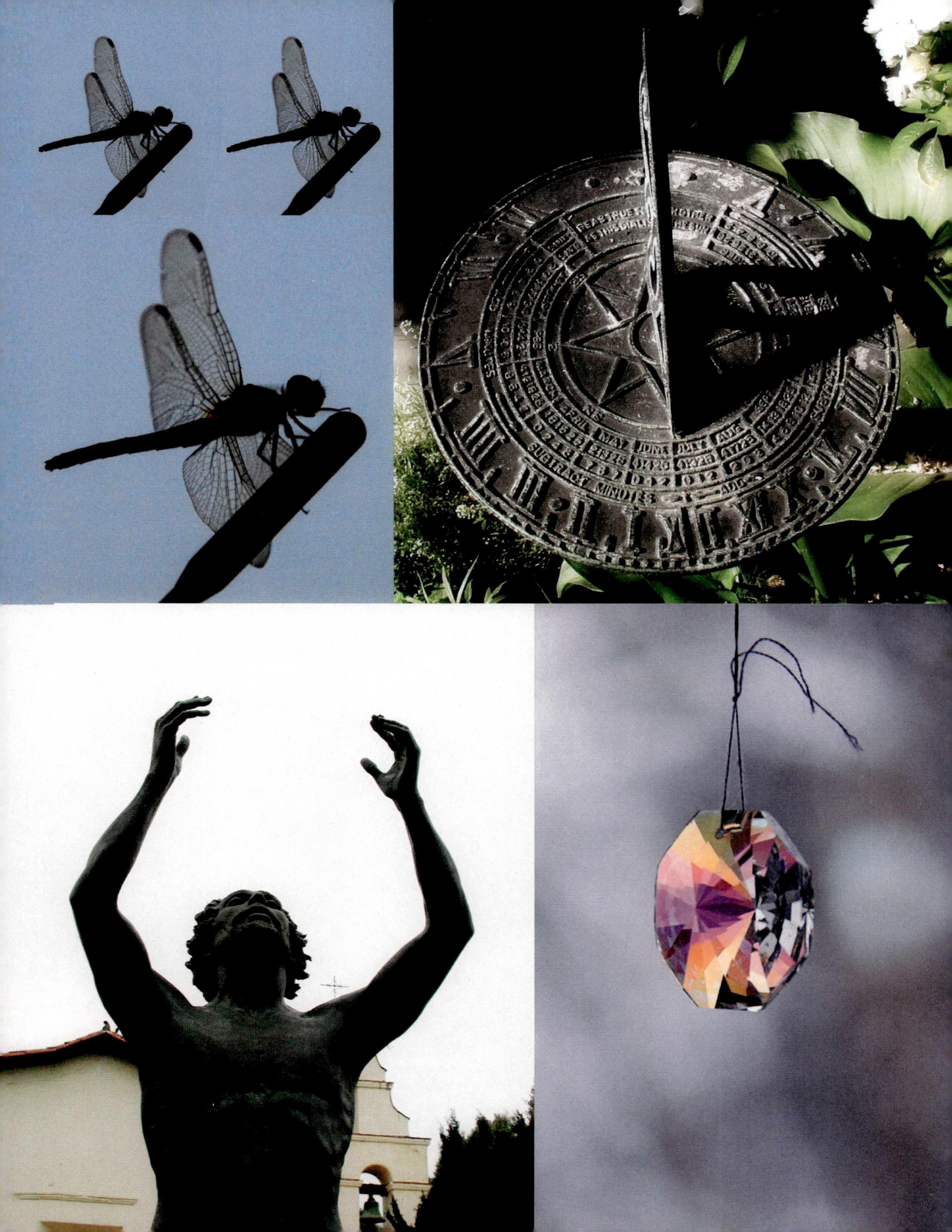
MAY
JUNE
JULY
AUG
SUBTRACT MINUTES
ADD

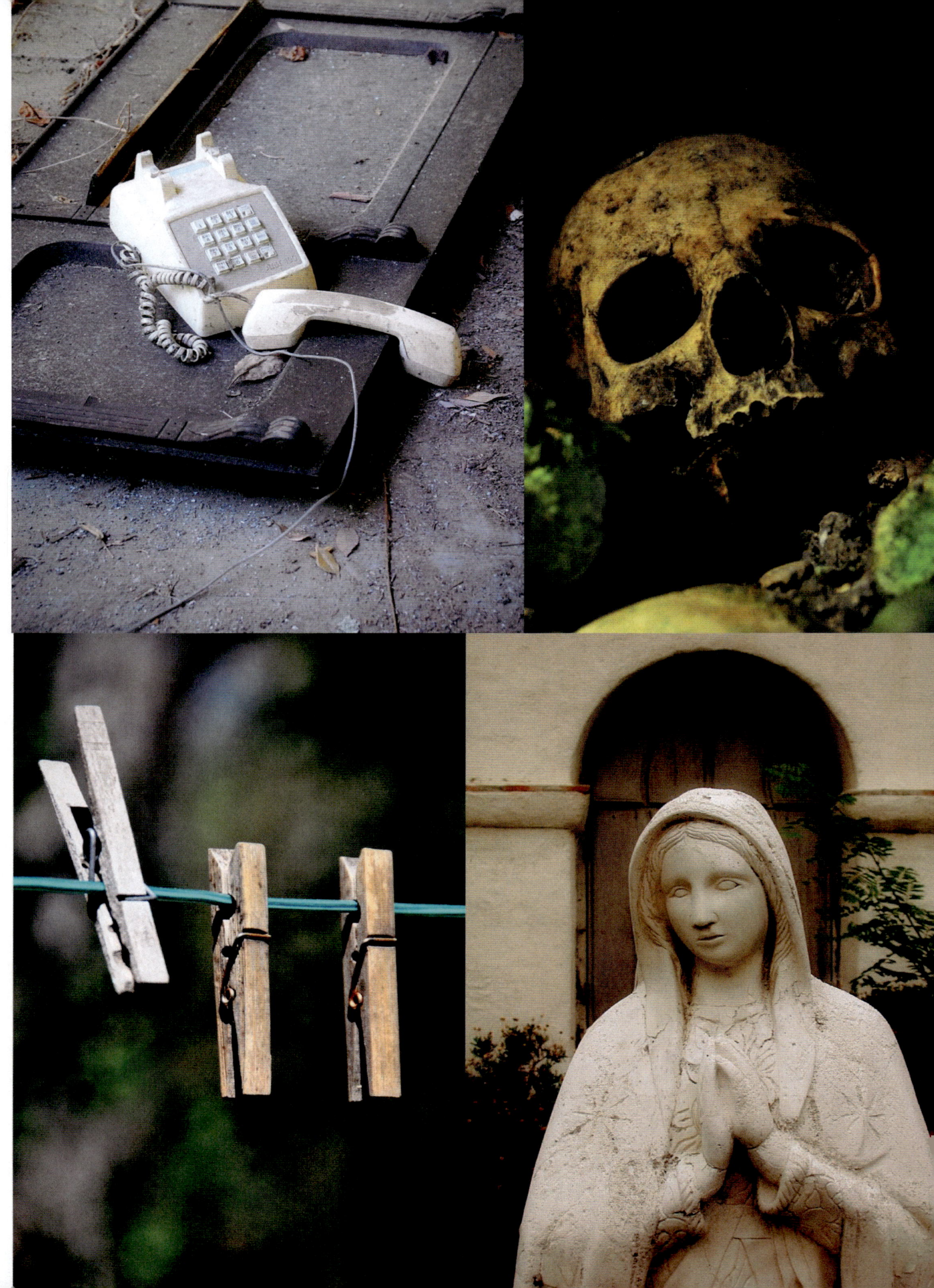

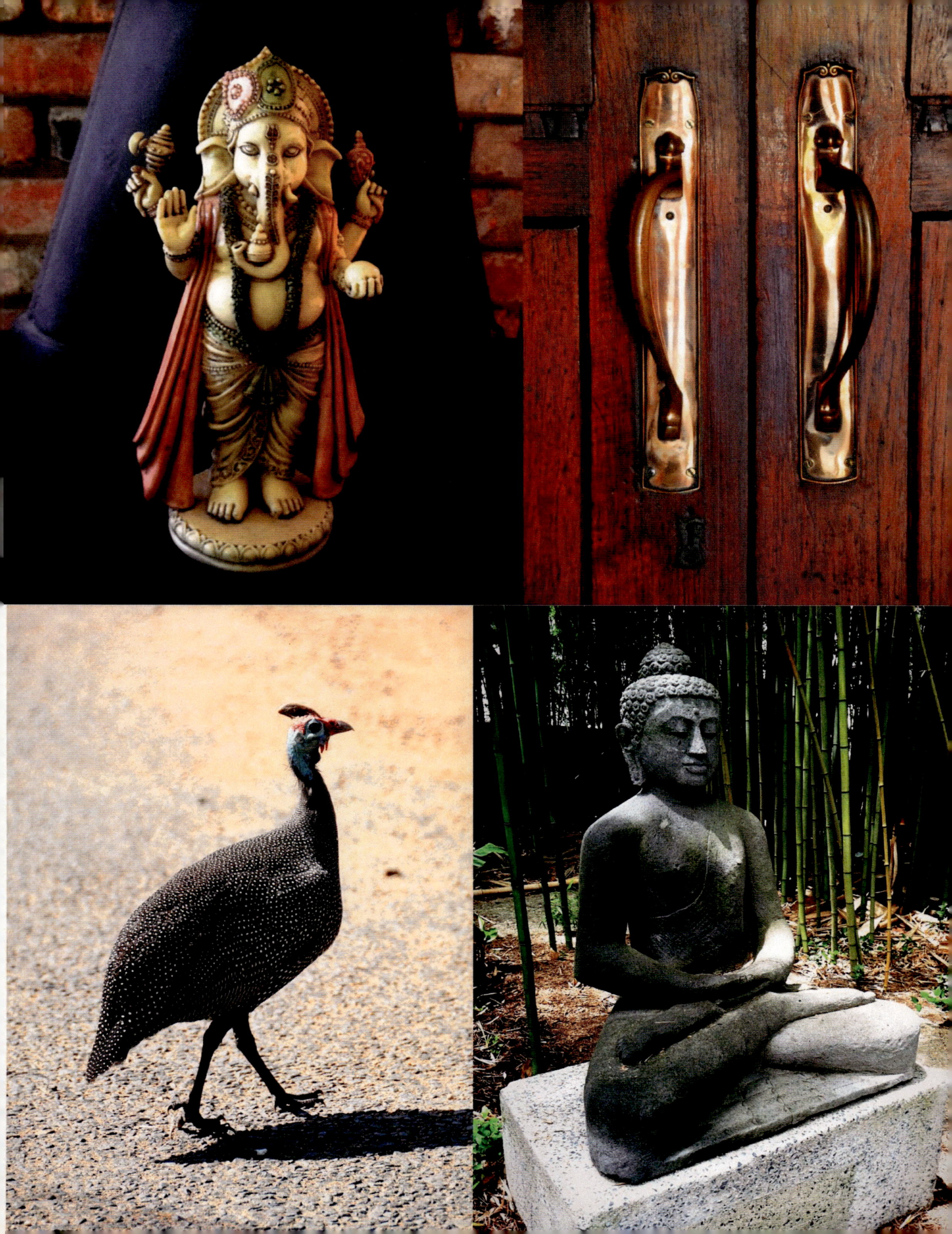

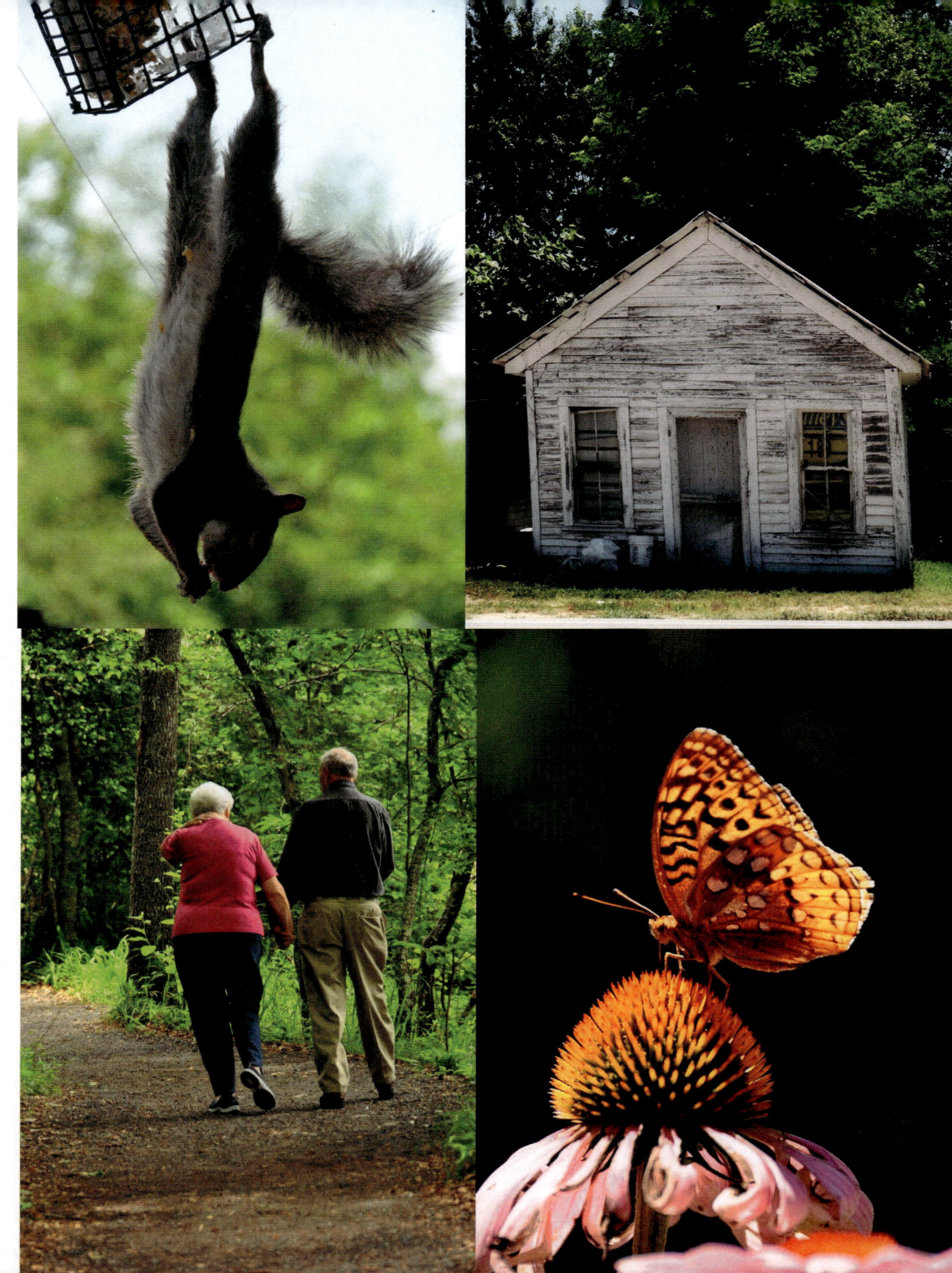

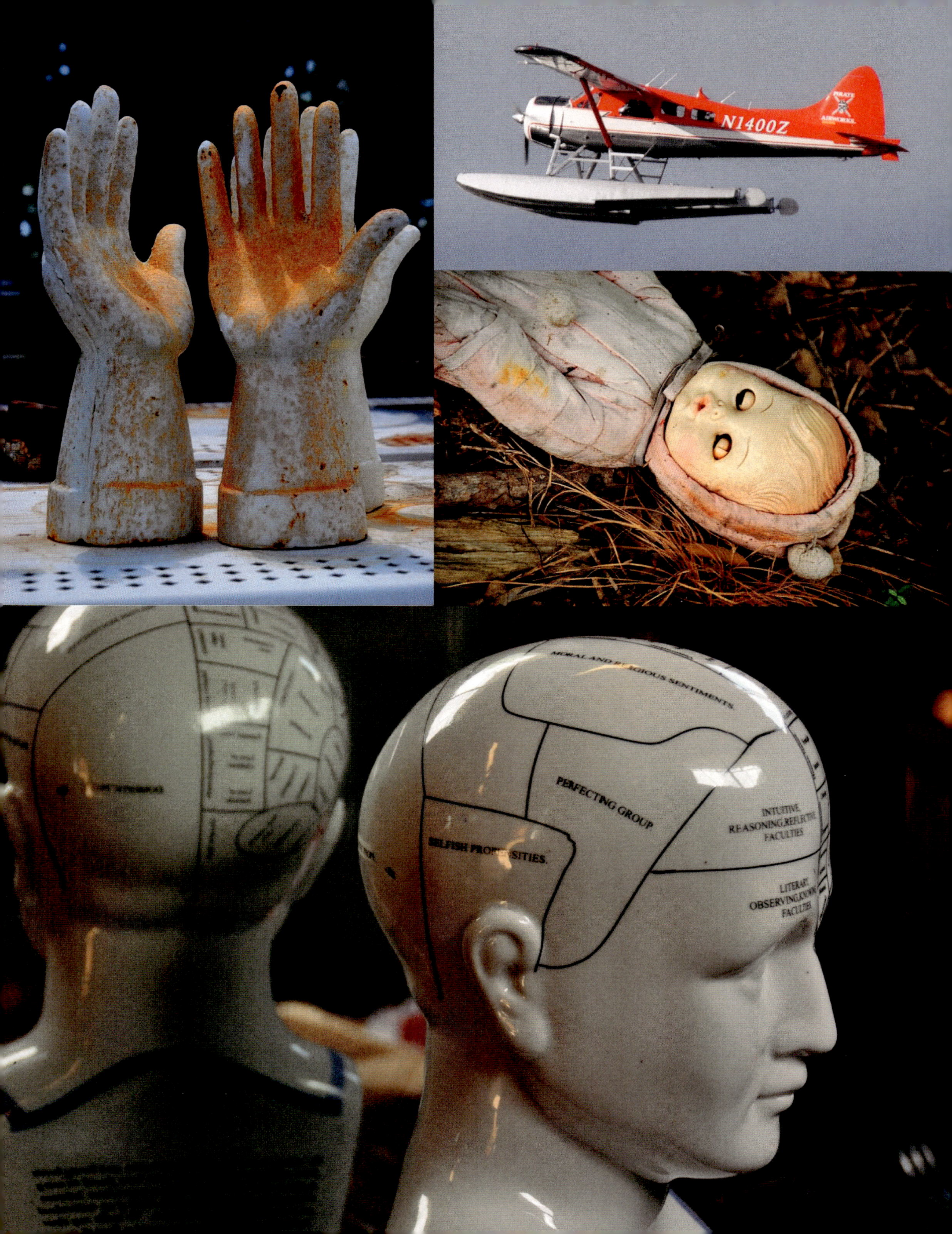
N1400Z
PERFECTING GROUP
INTUITIVE,
FACULTIES
LITERARY,
FACULTIES

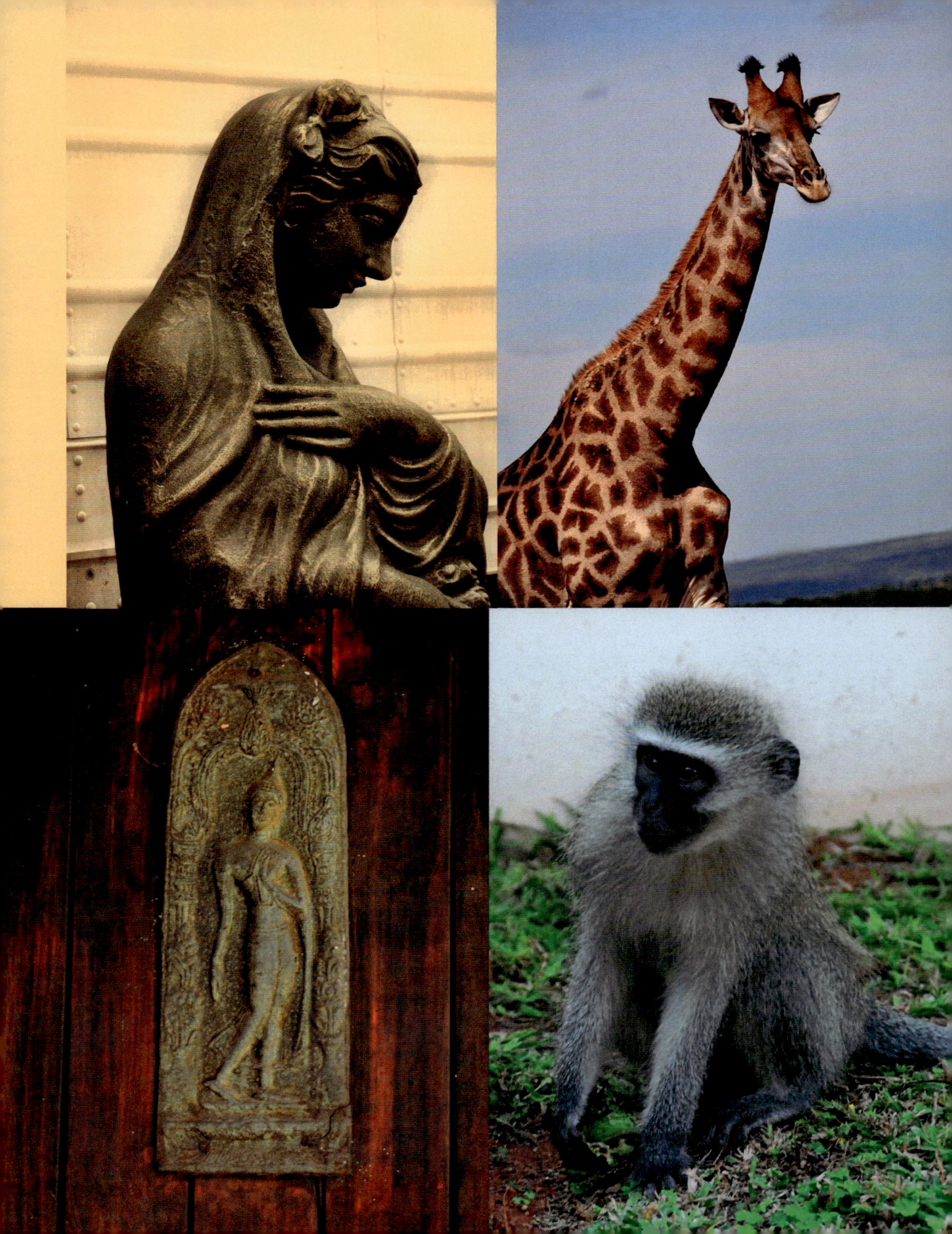

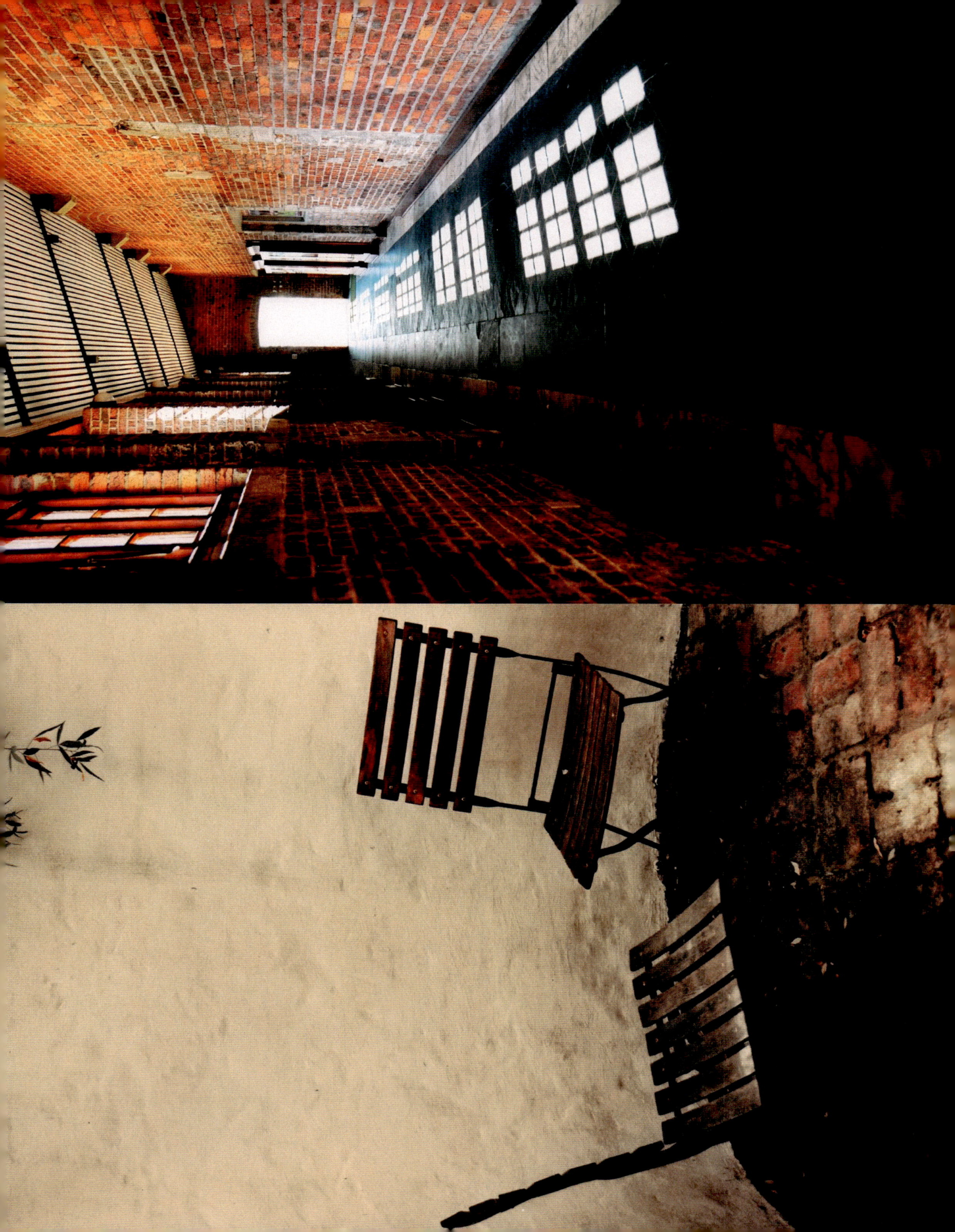

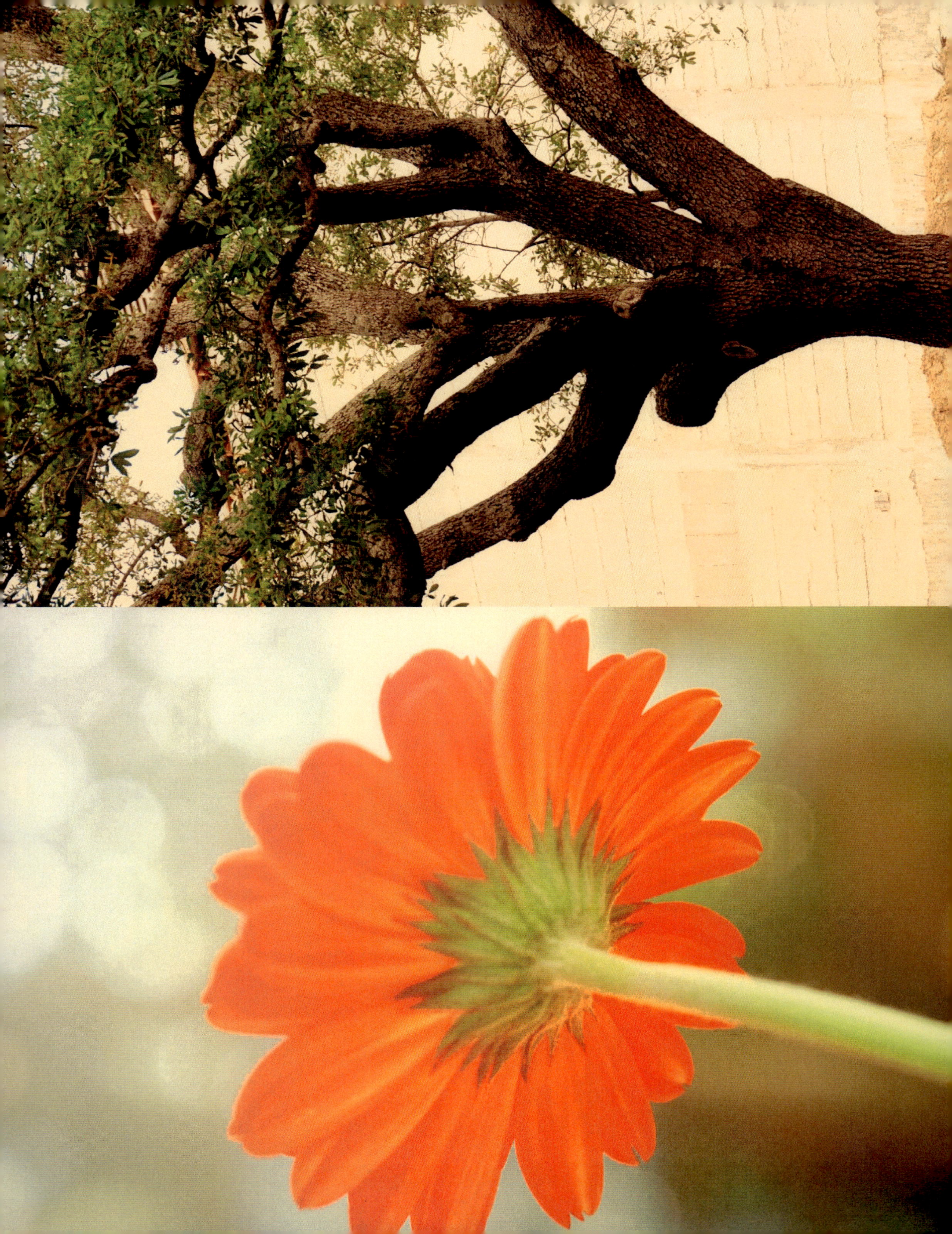

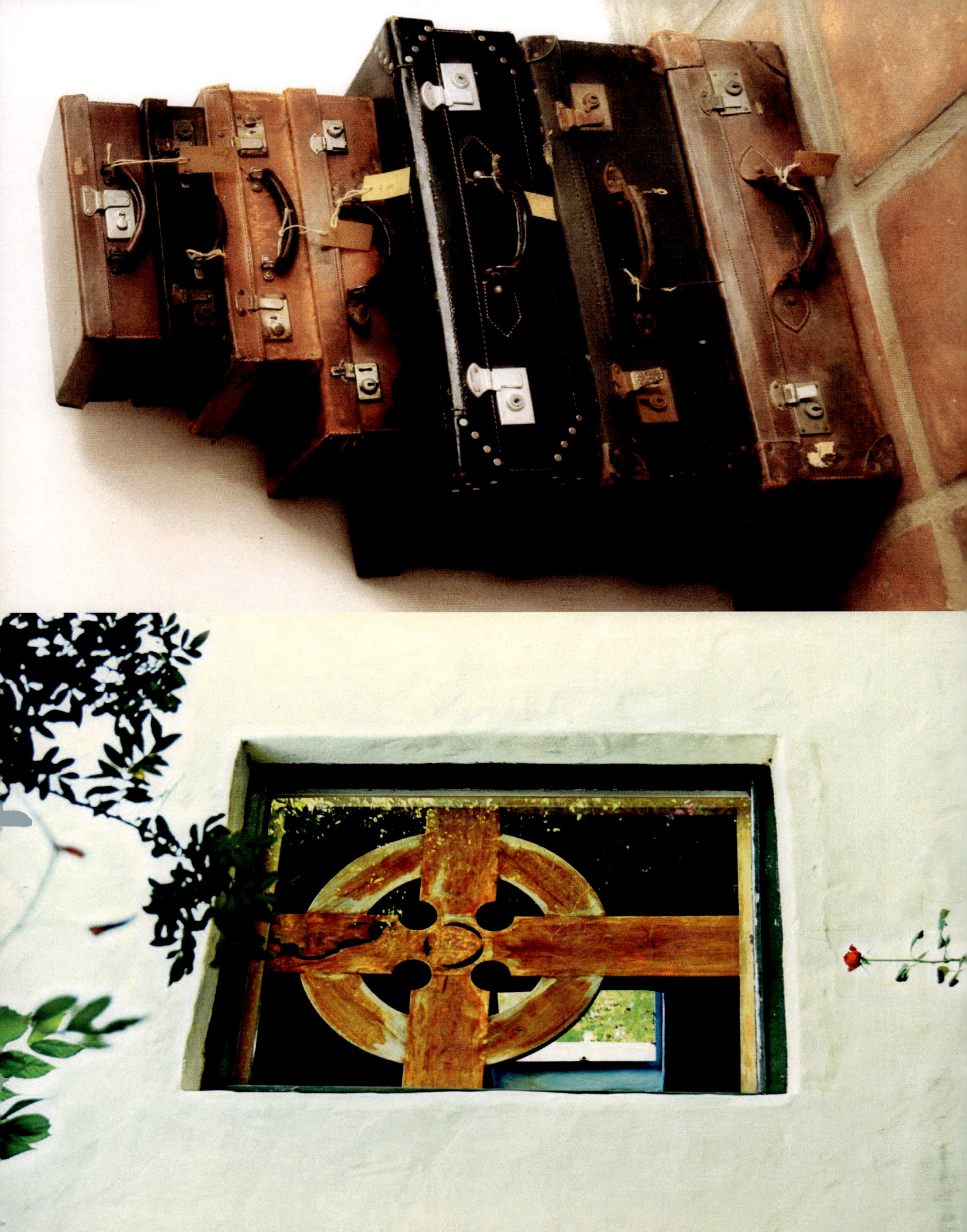

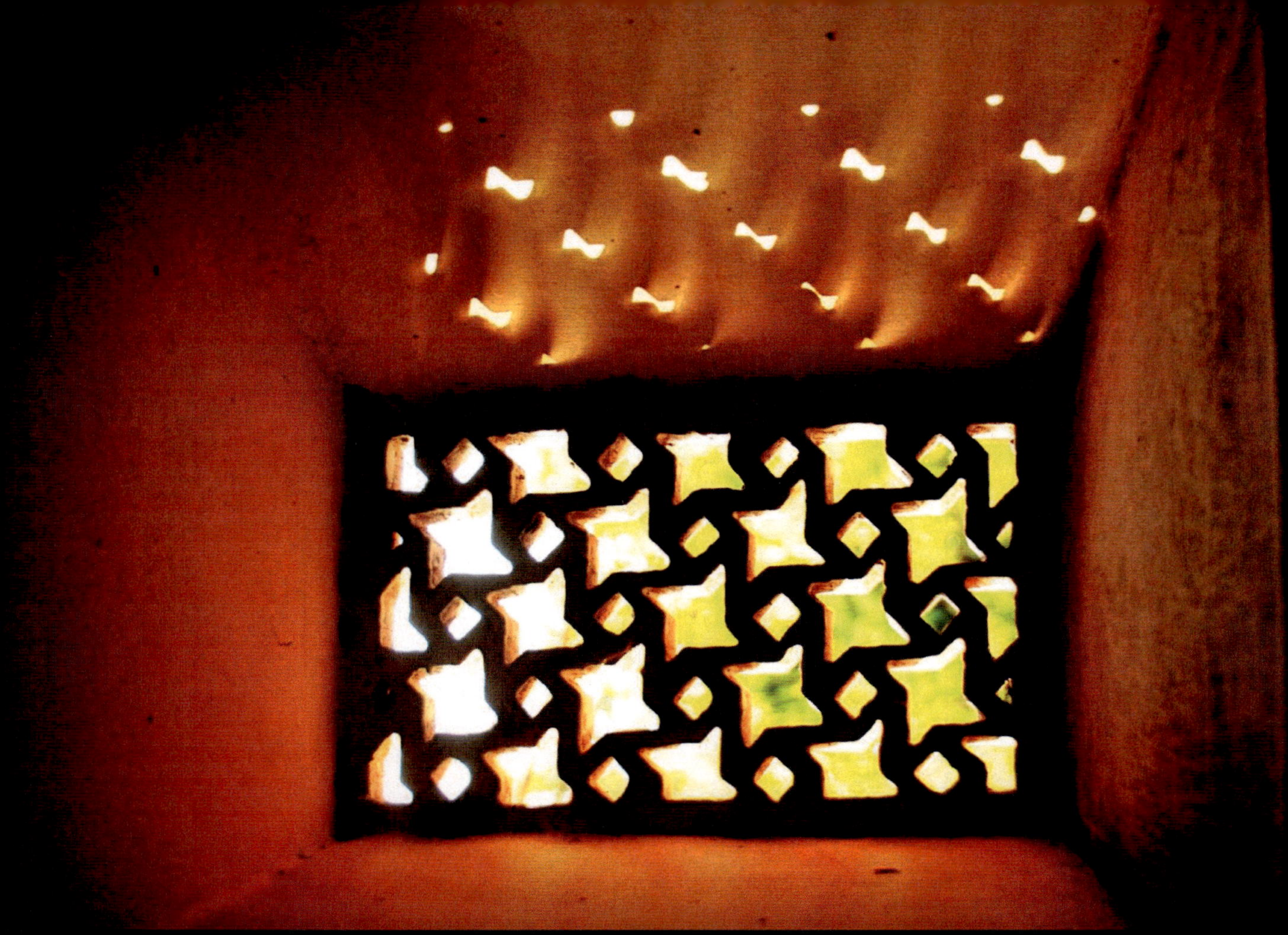

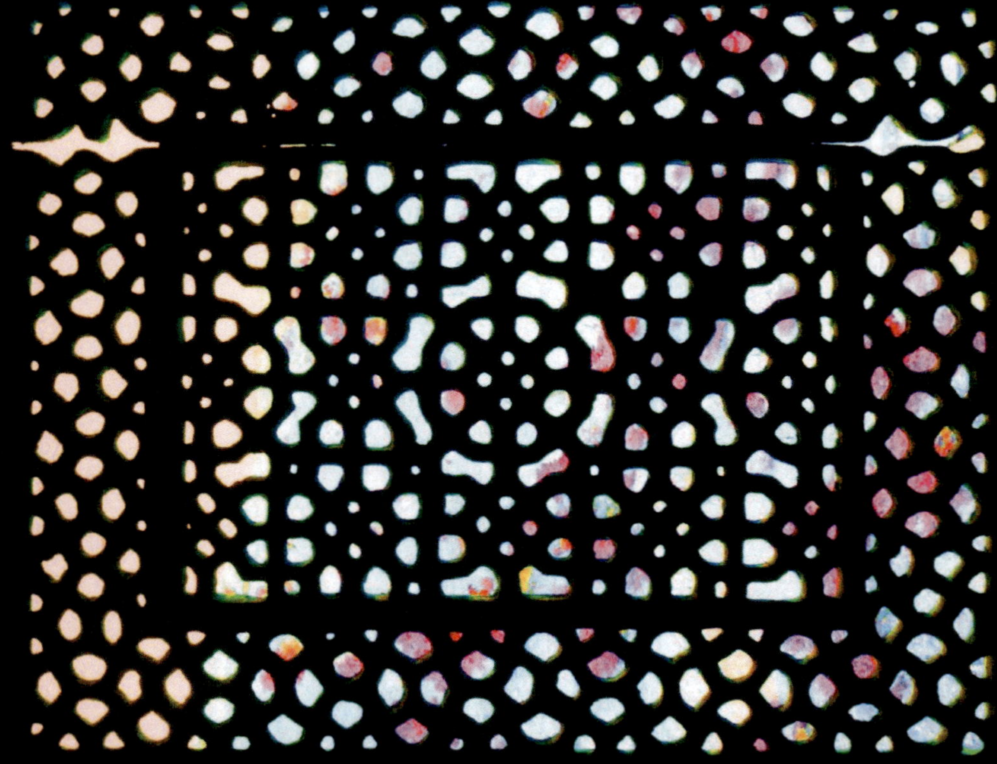

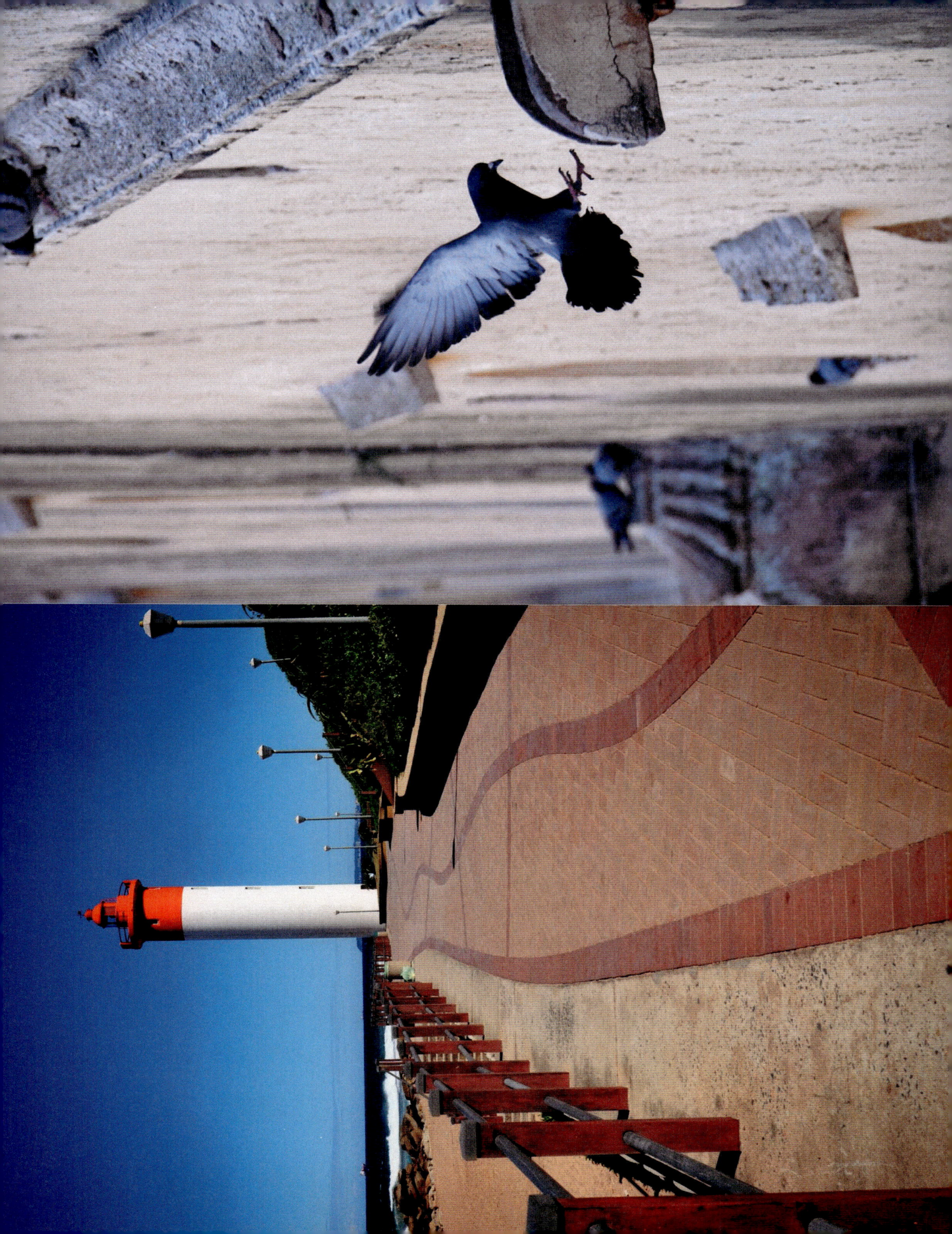

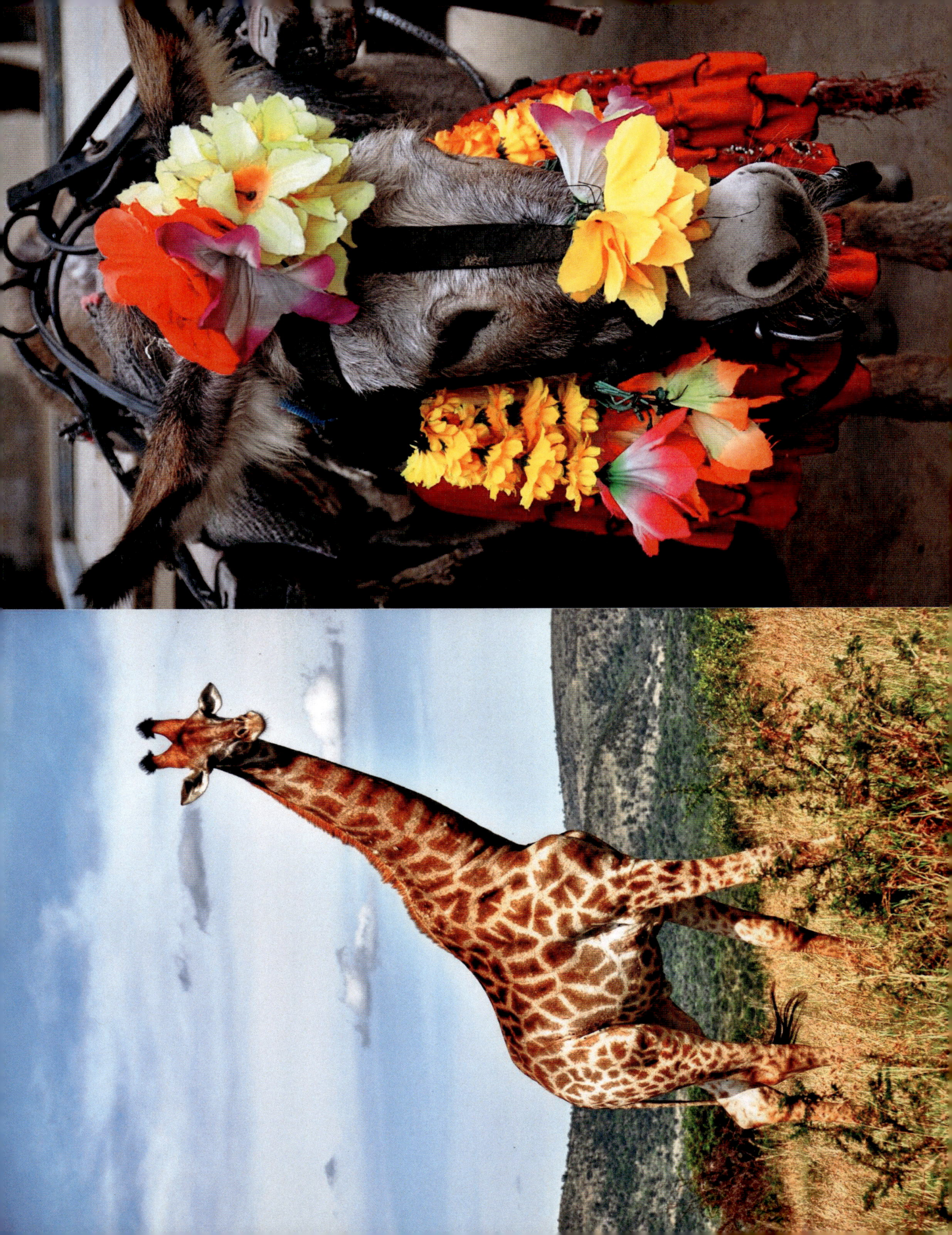

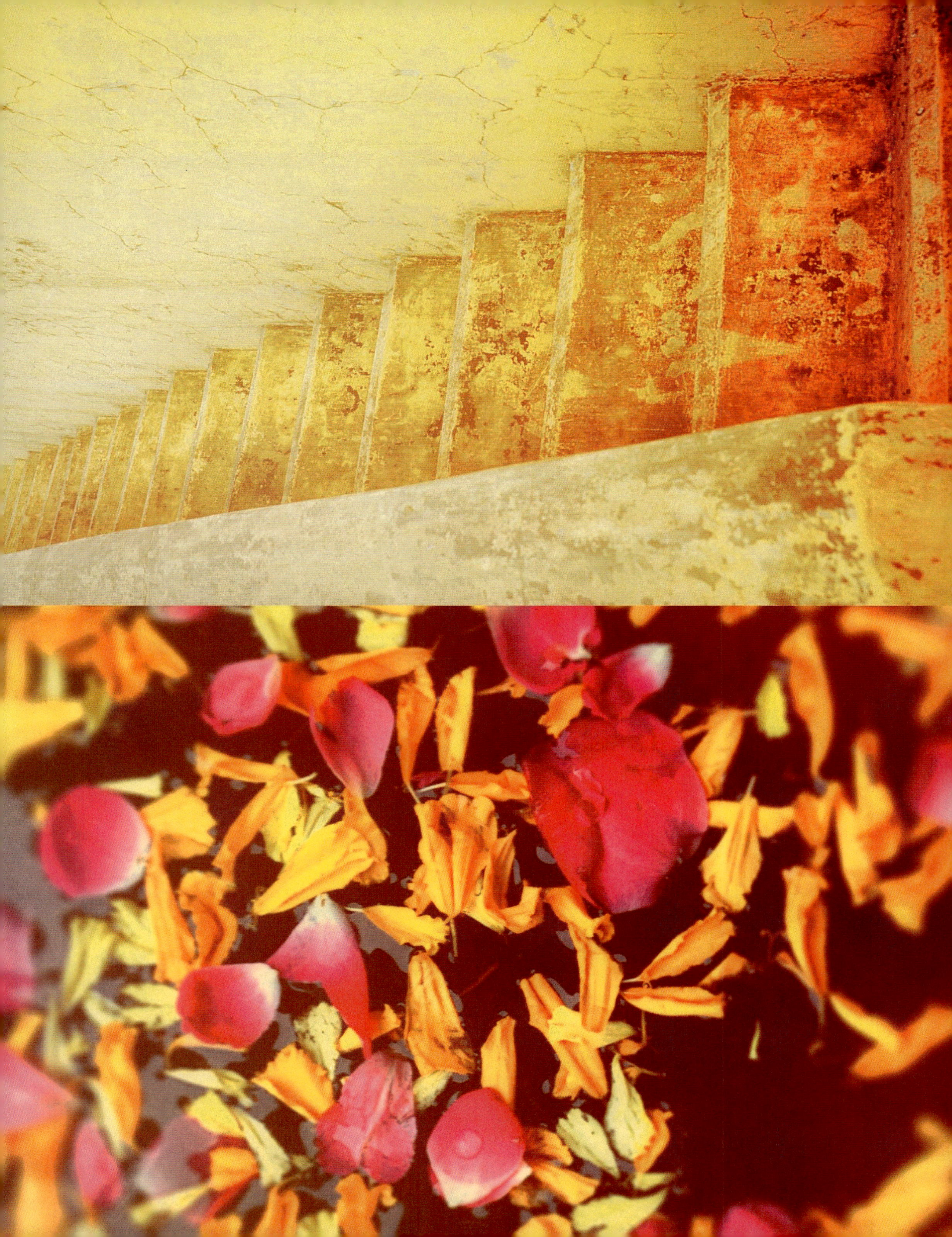

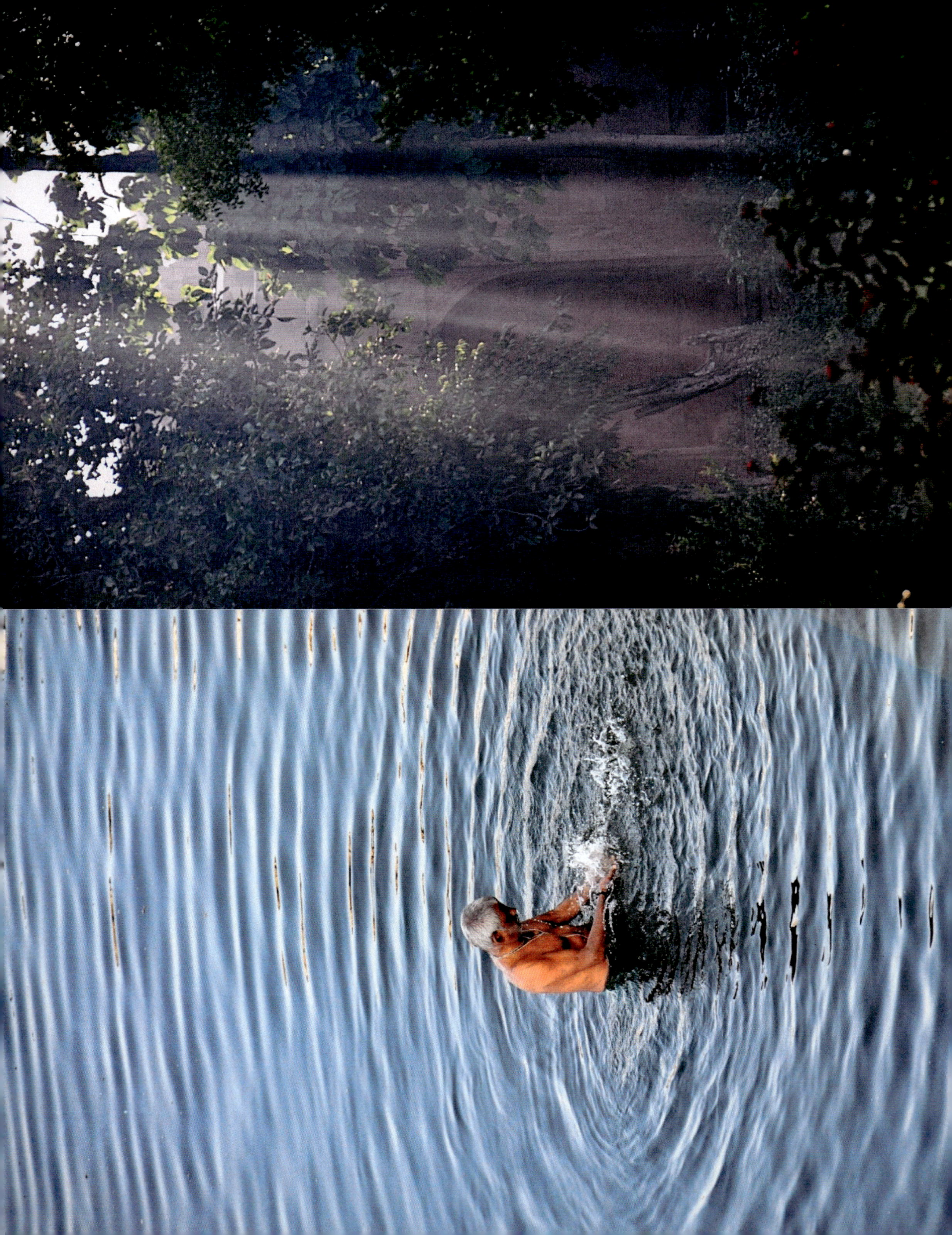

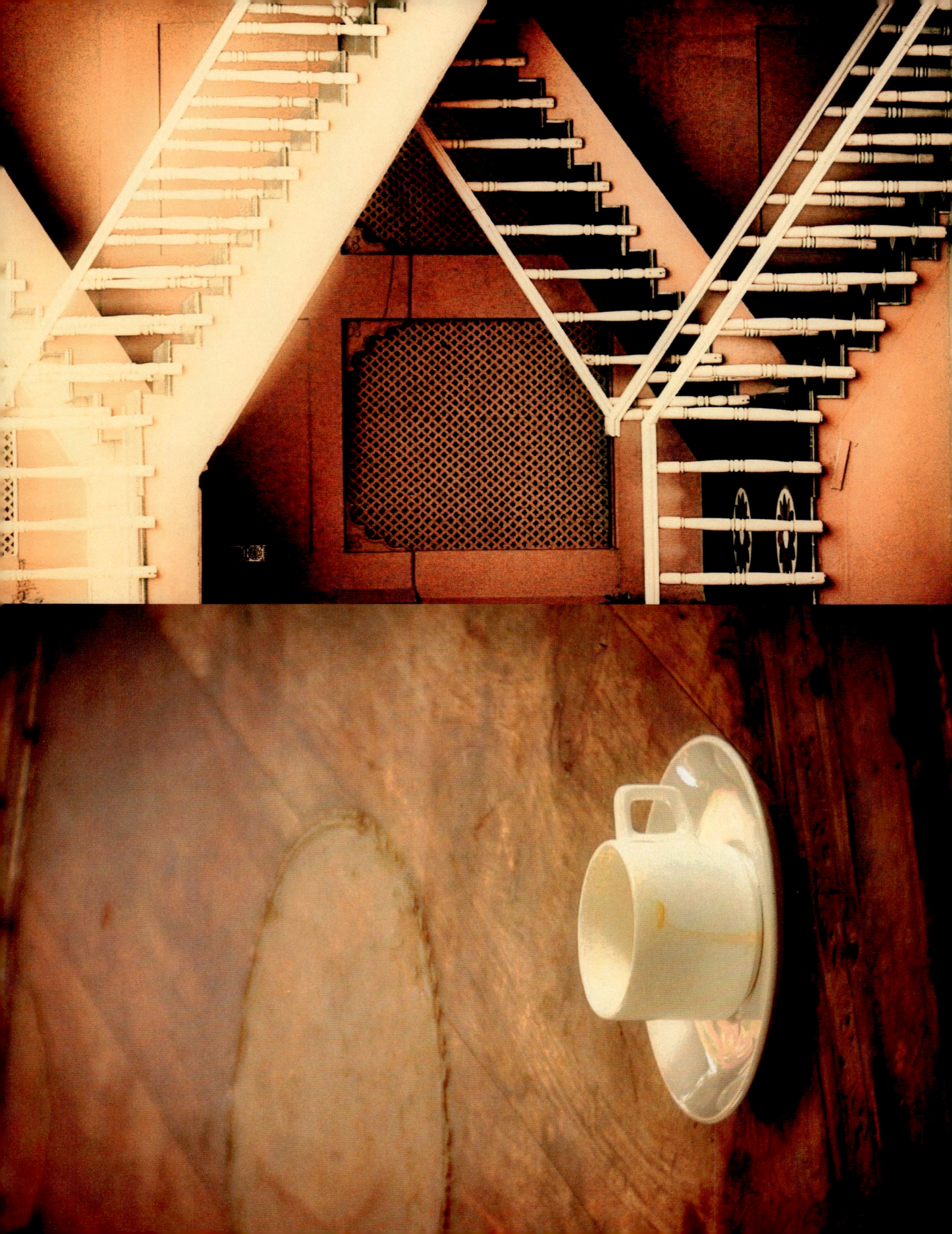

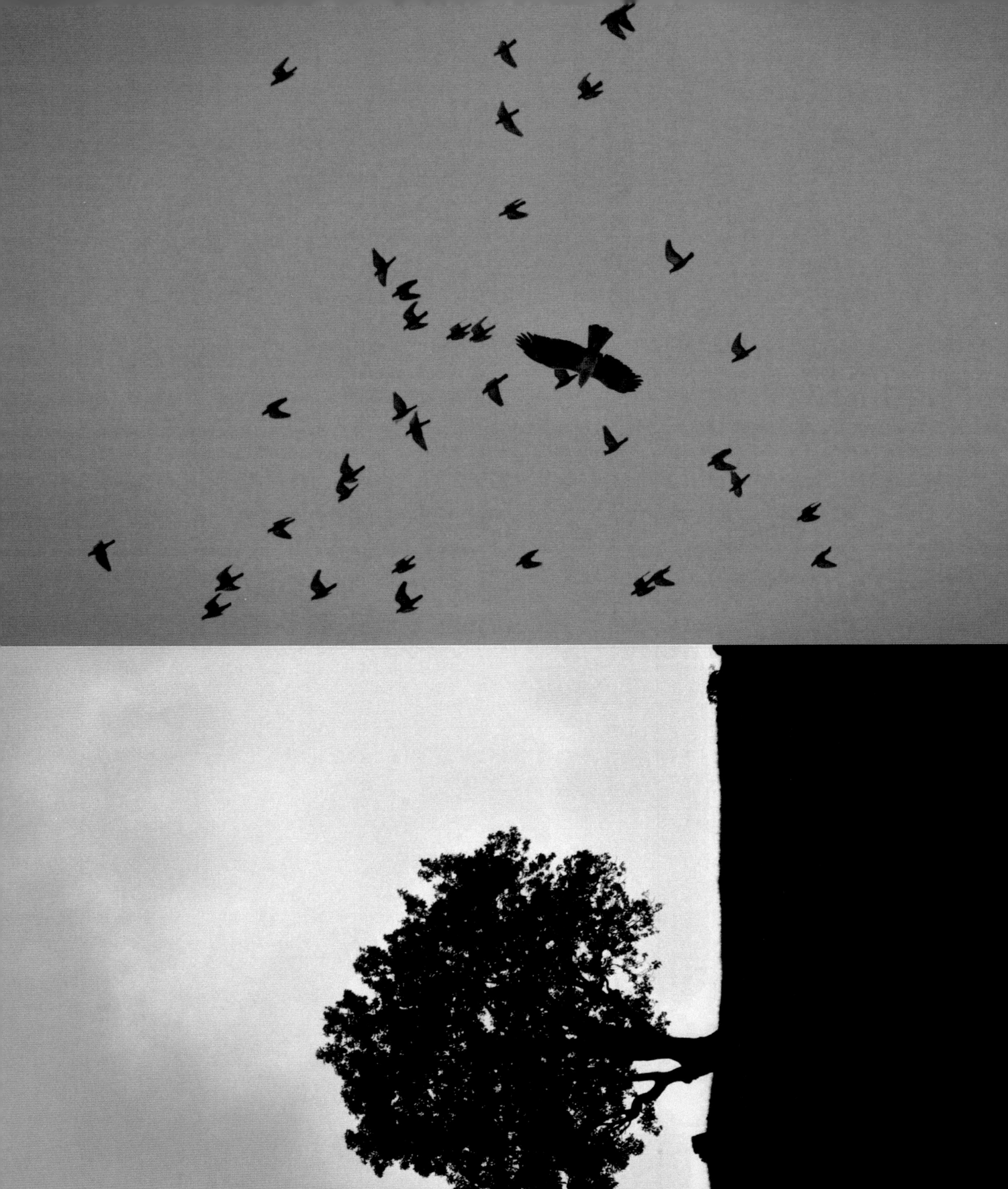

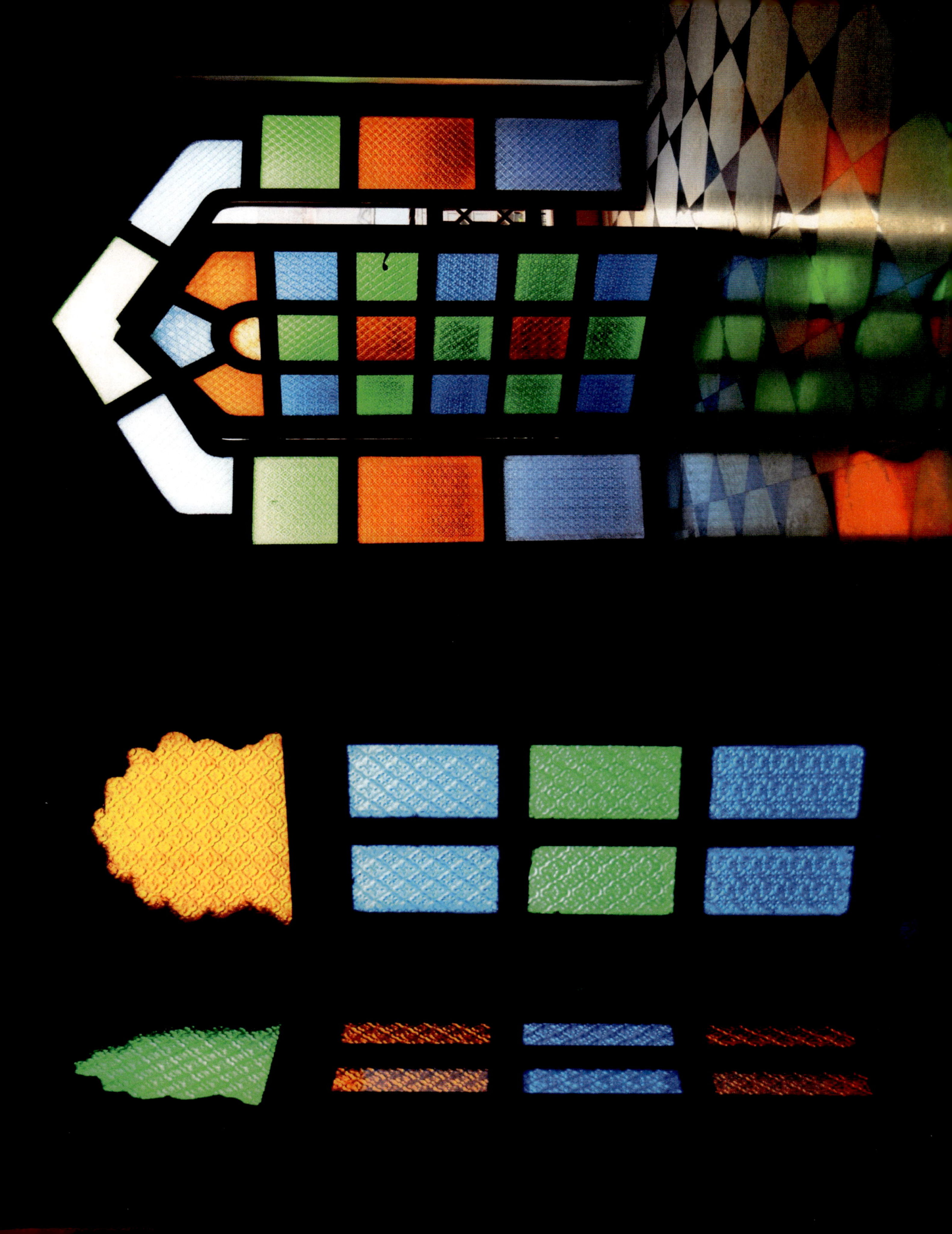

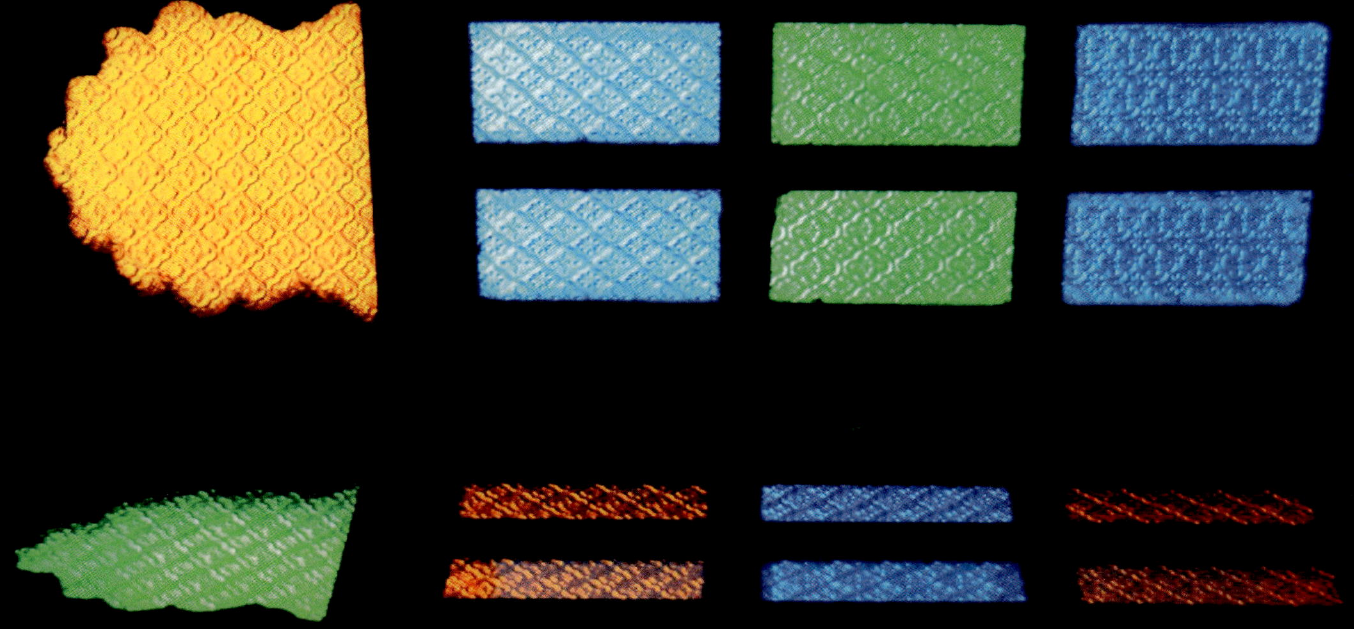

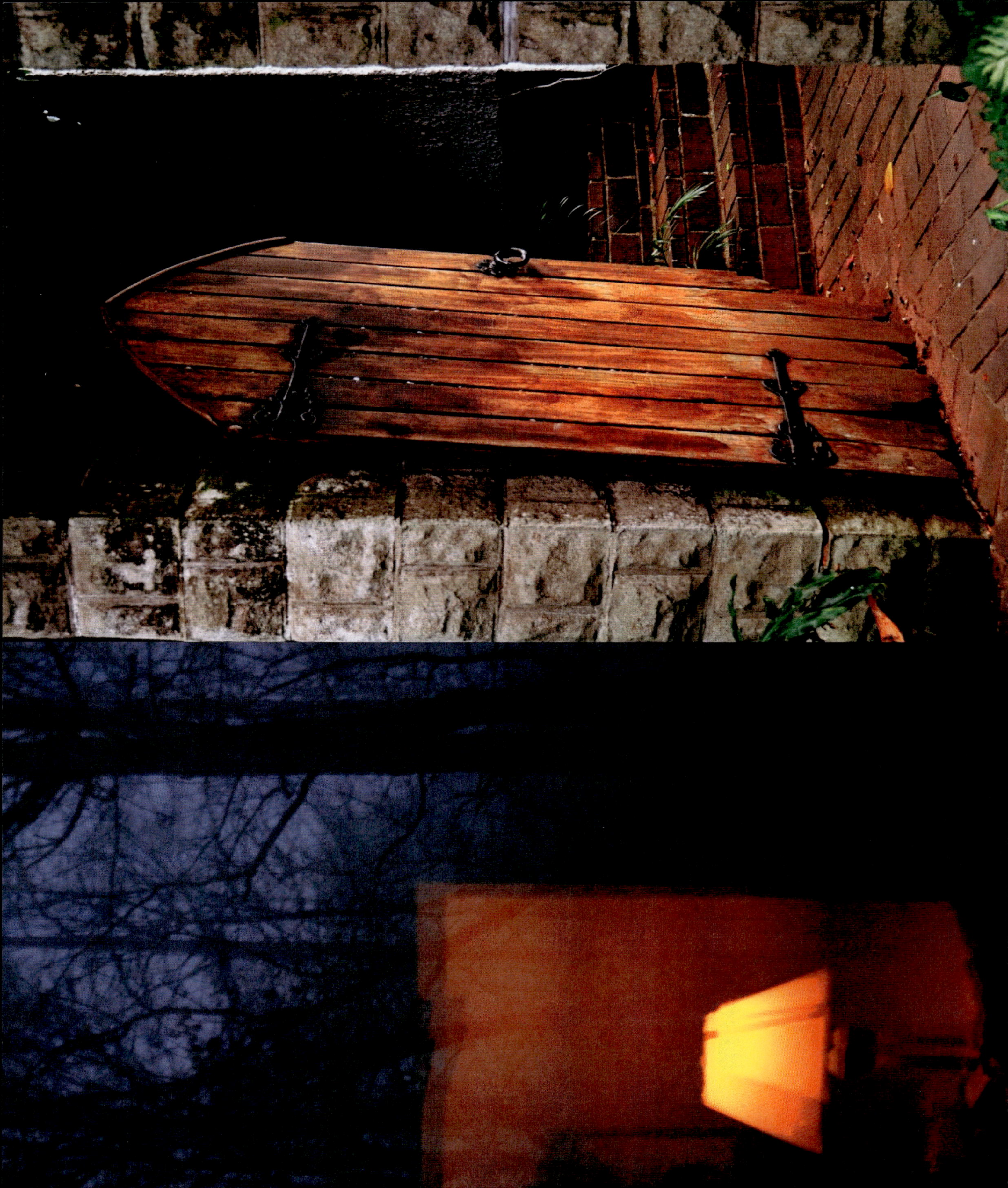

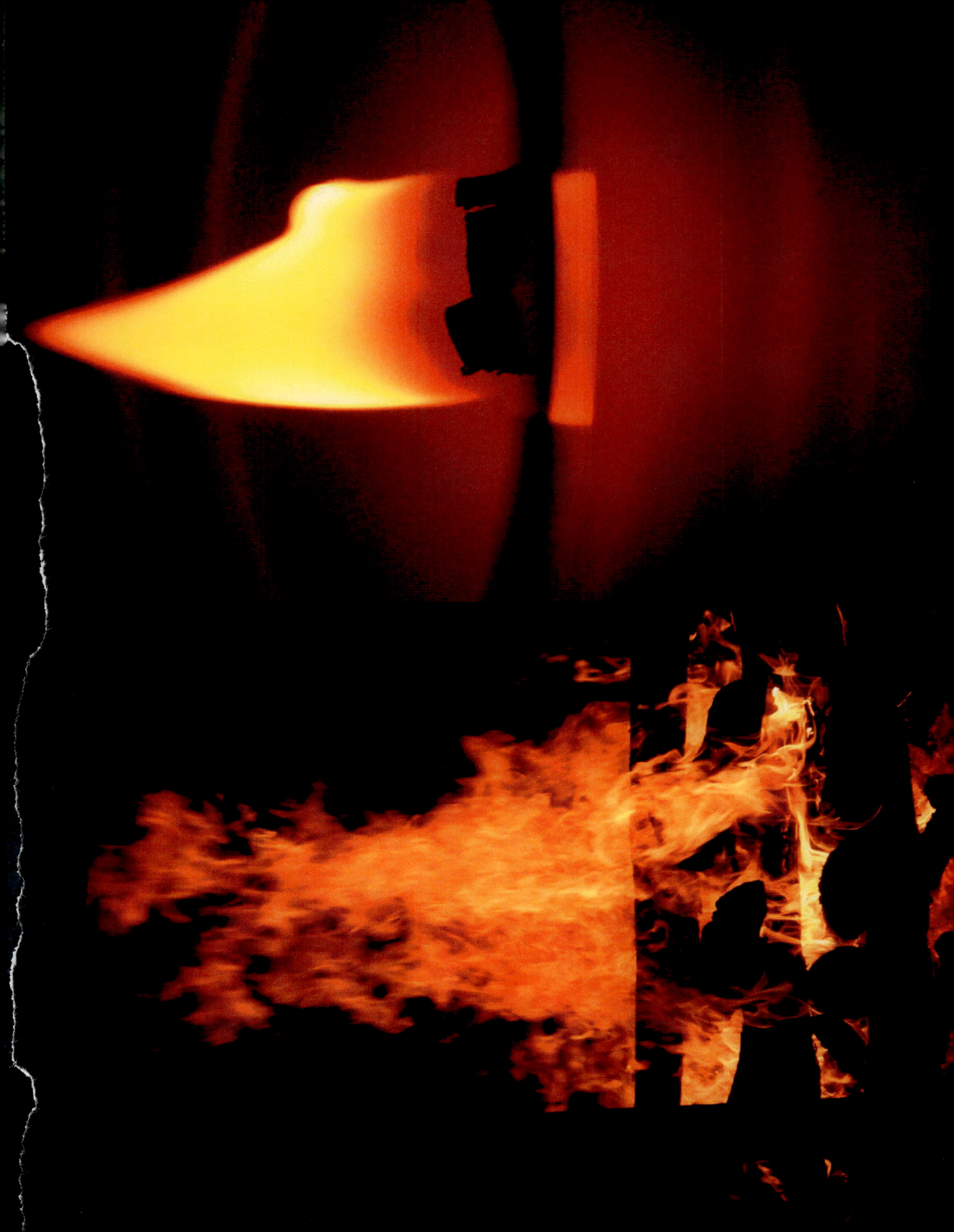

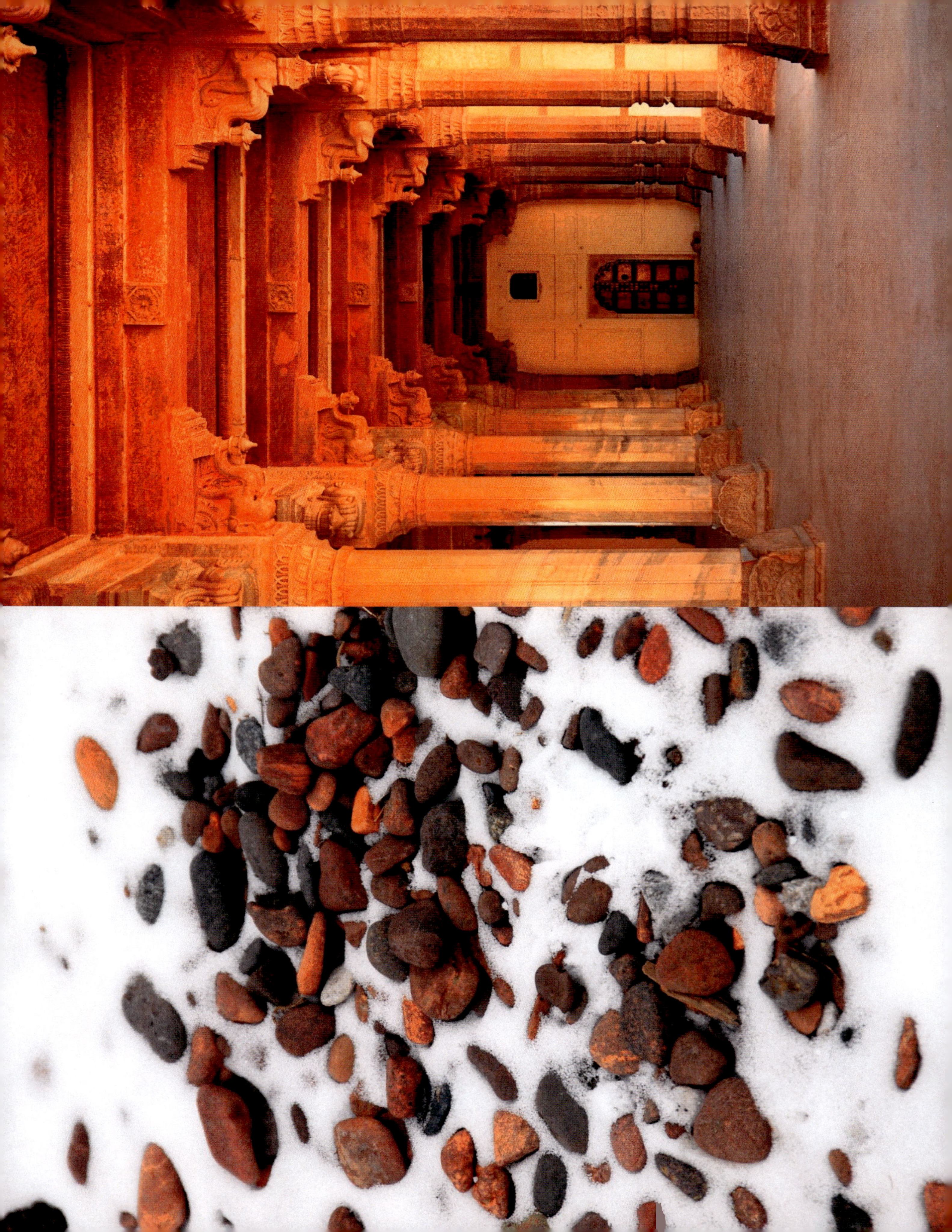

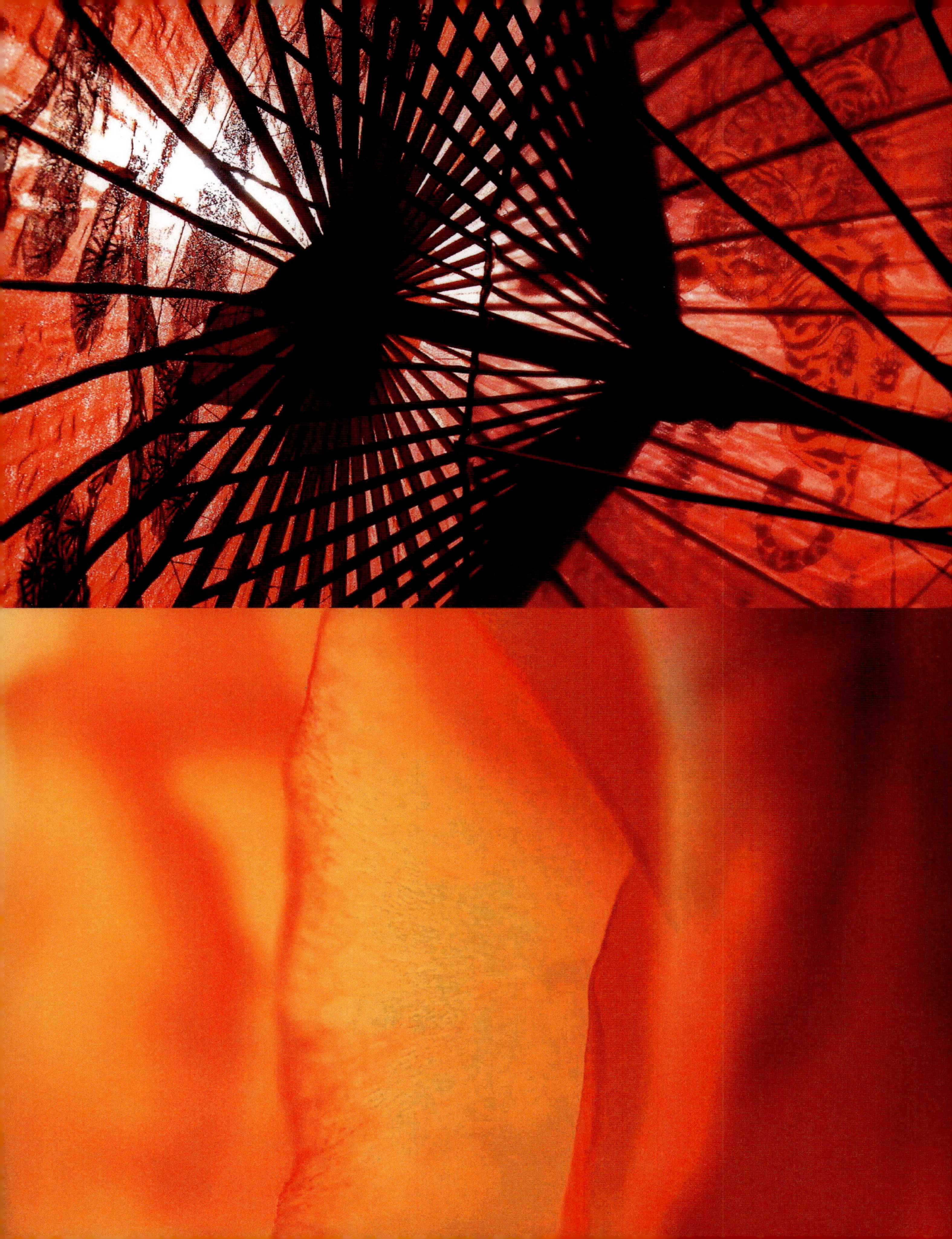

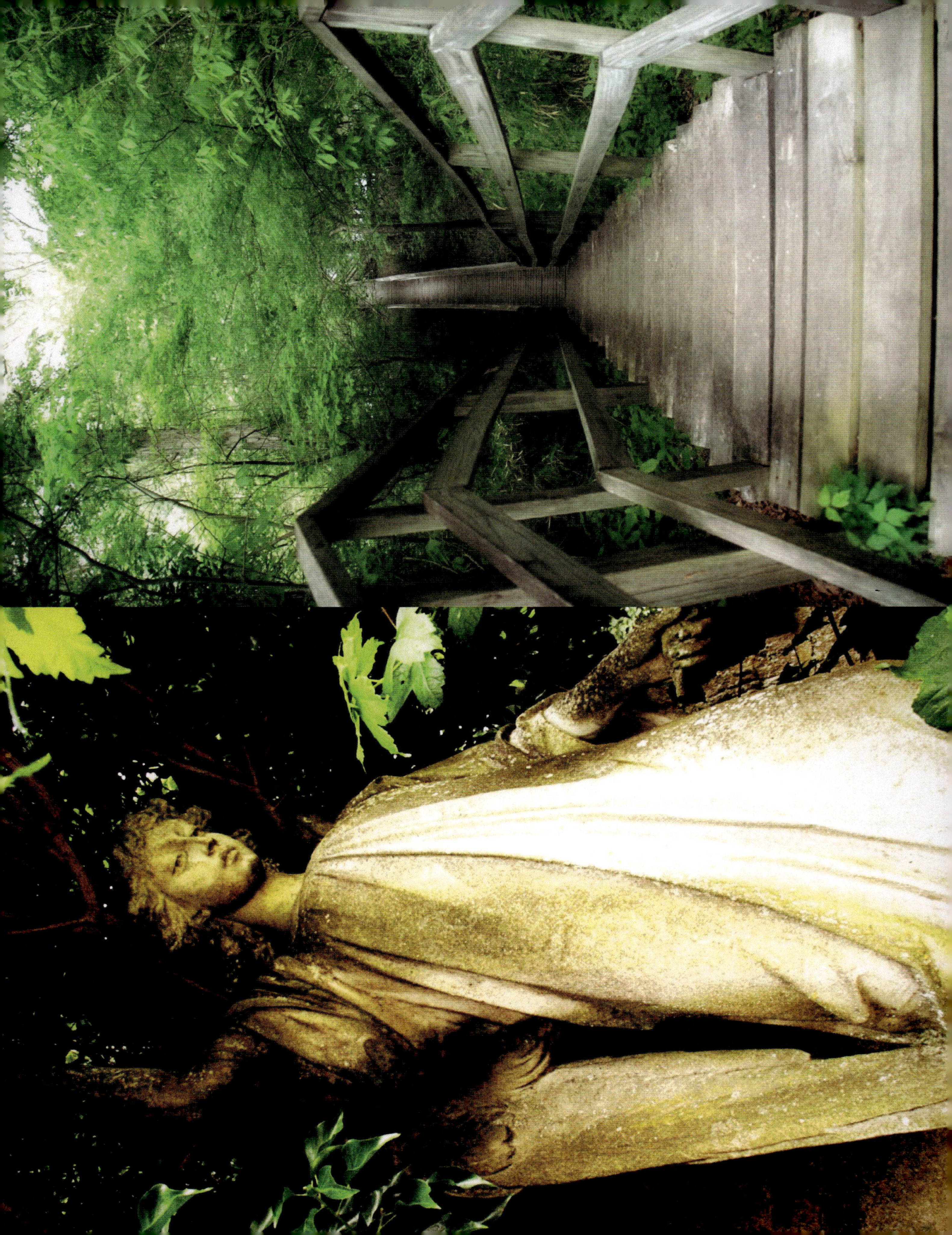

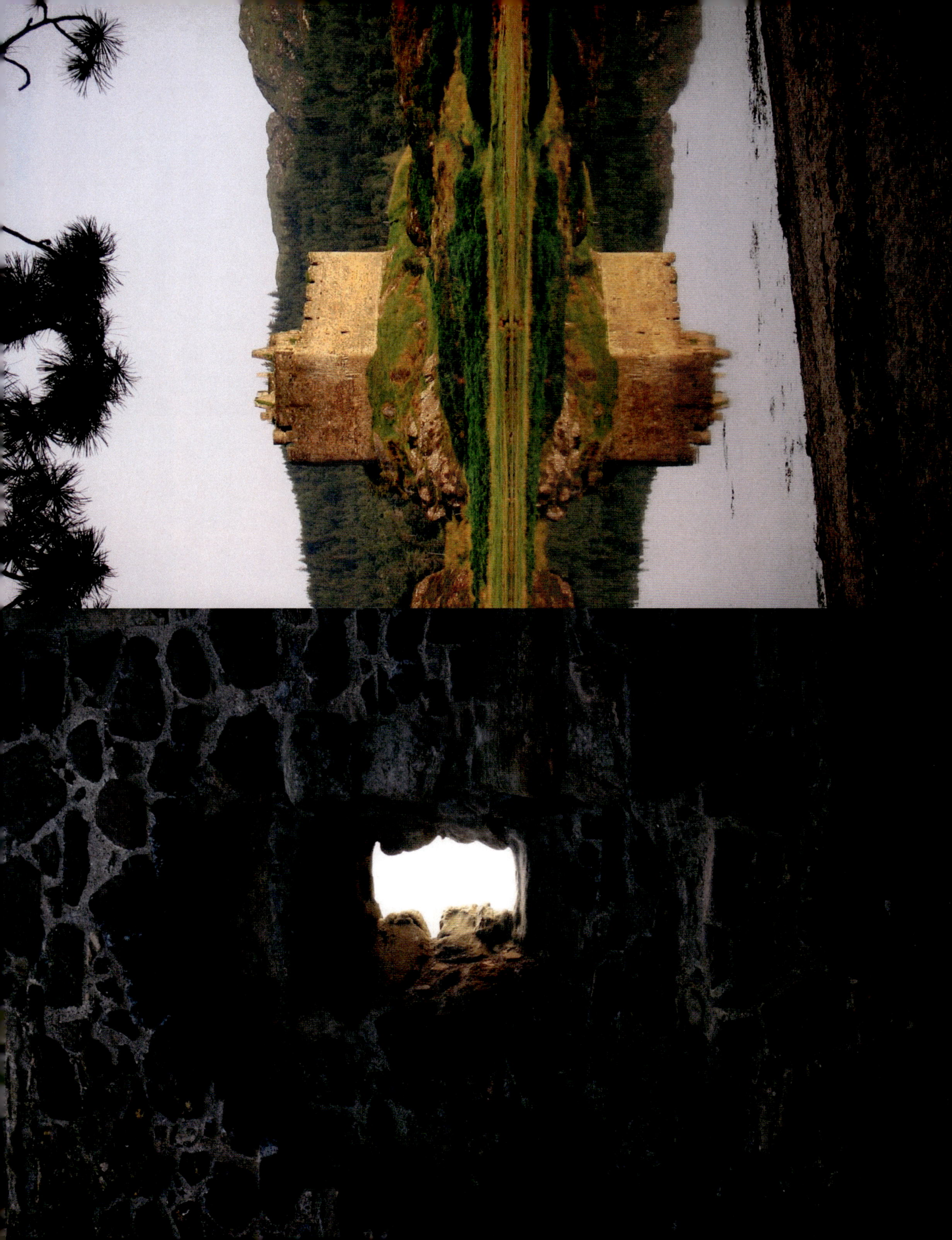

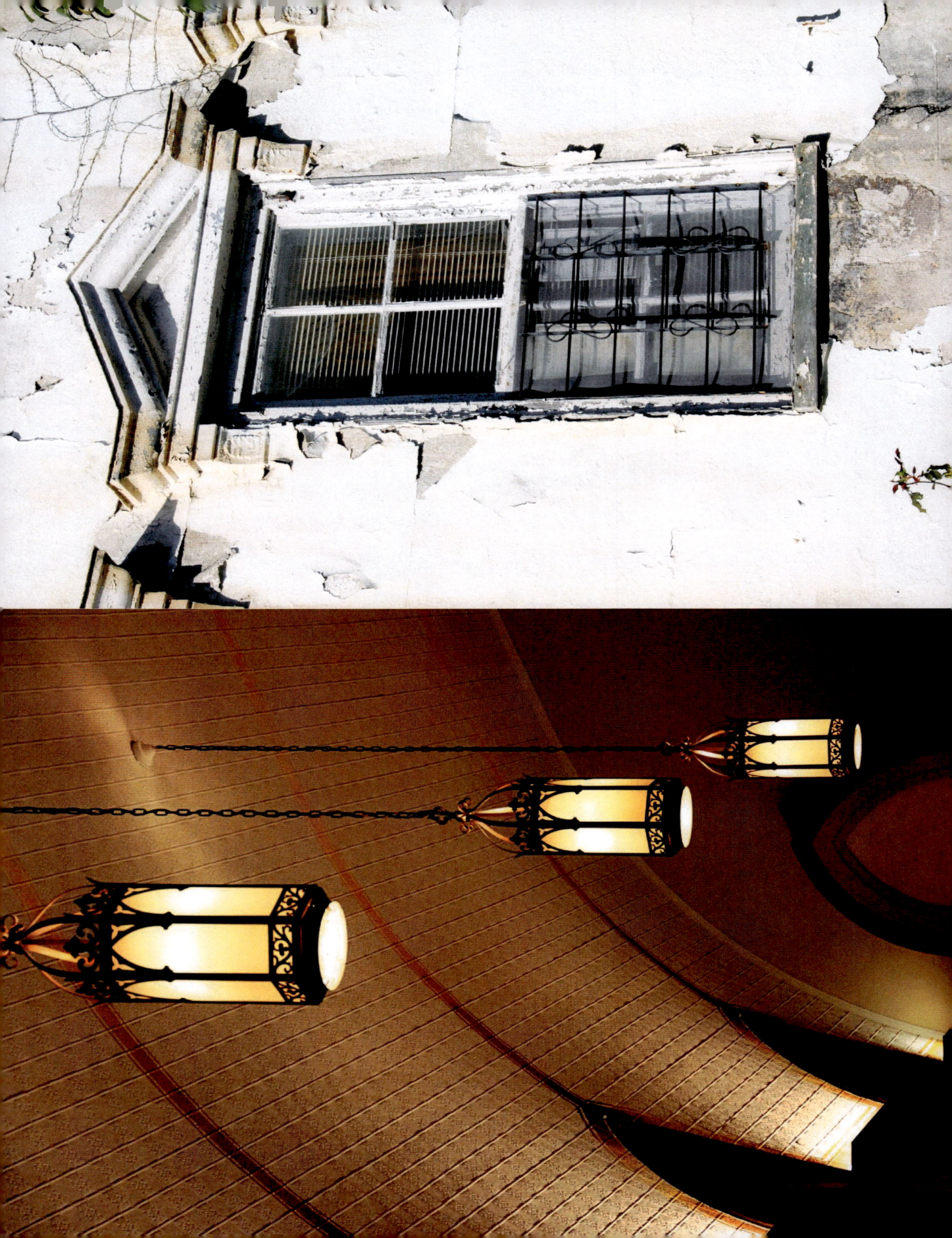

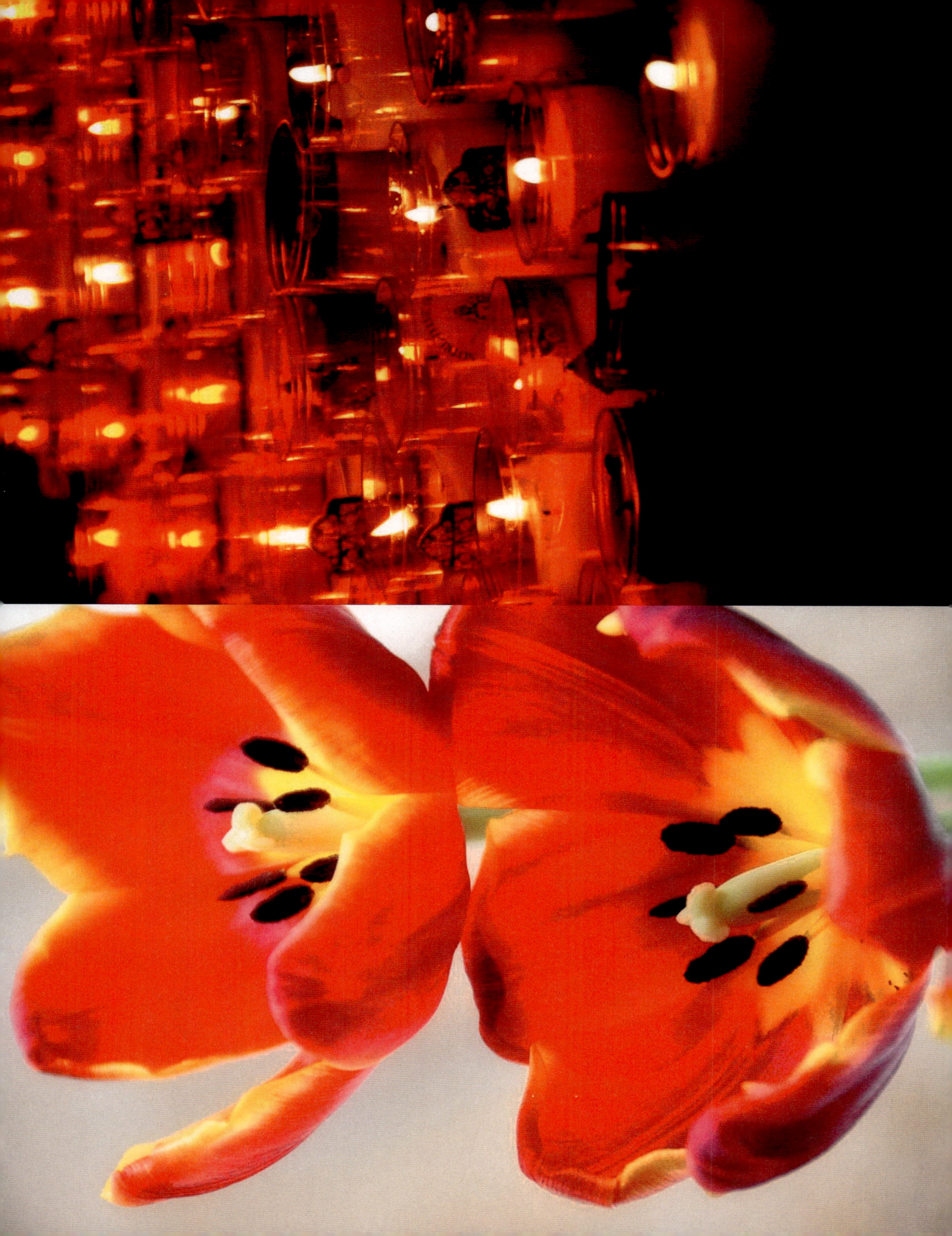

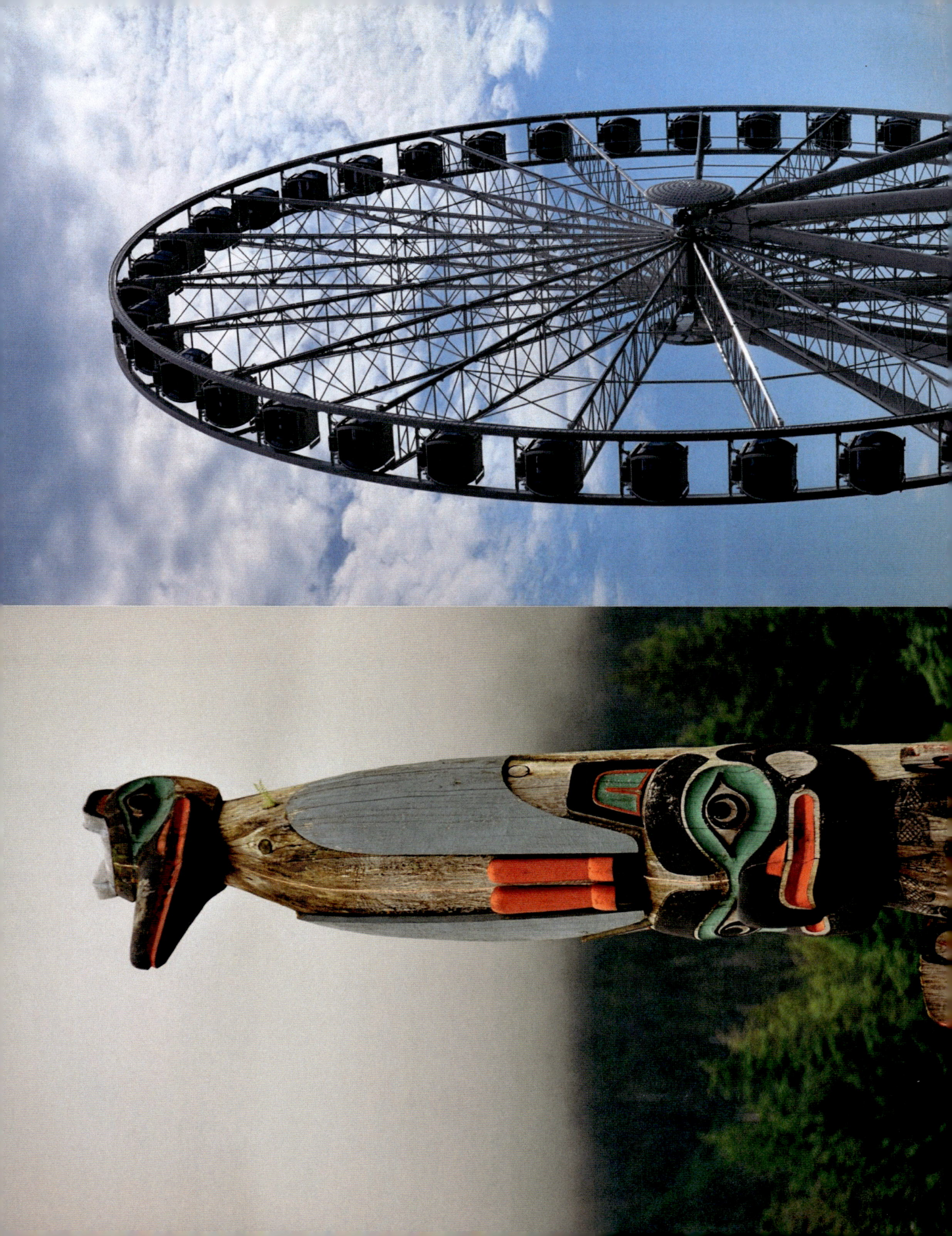

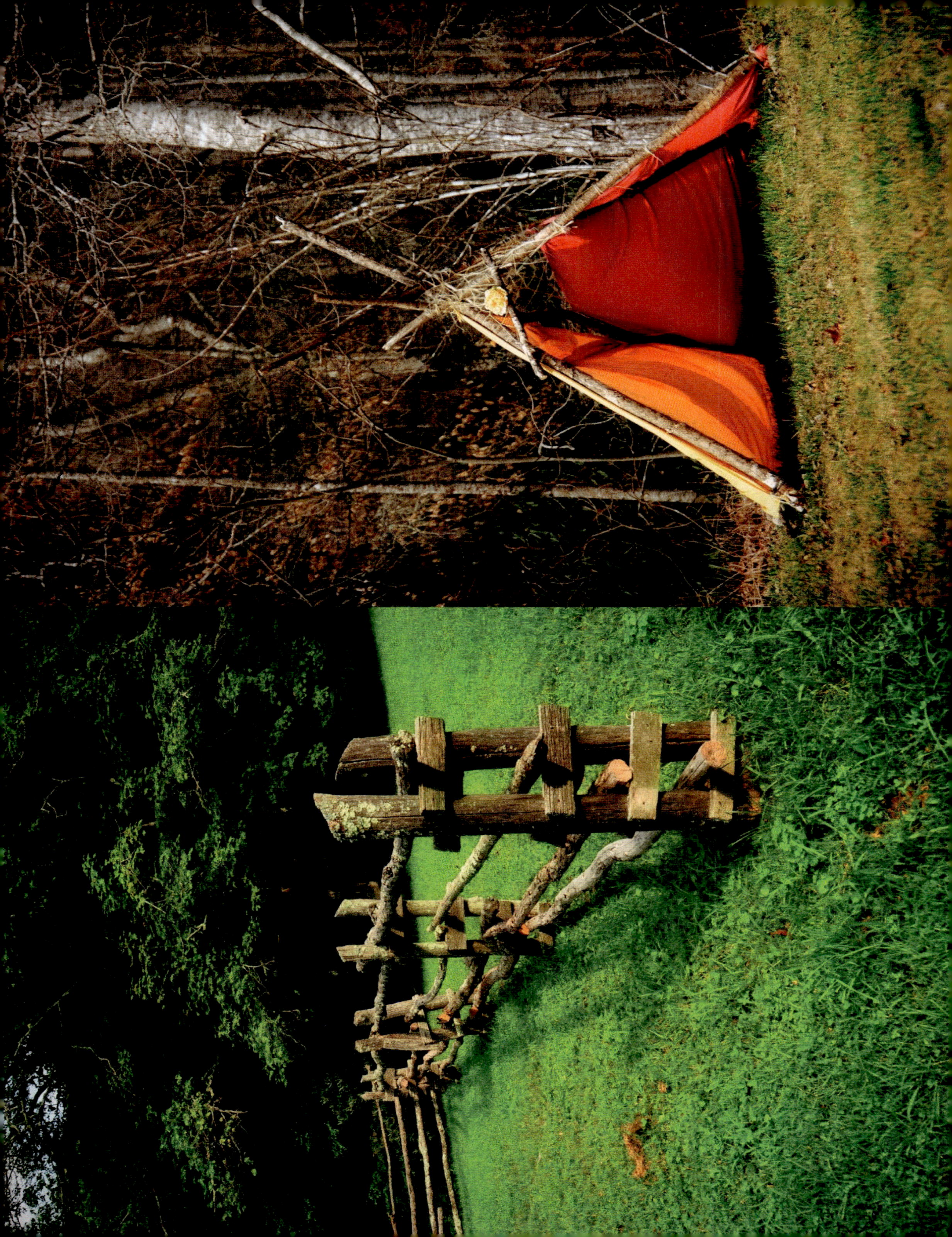

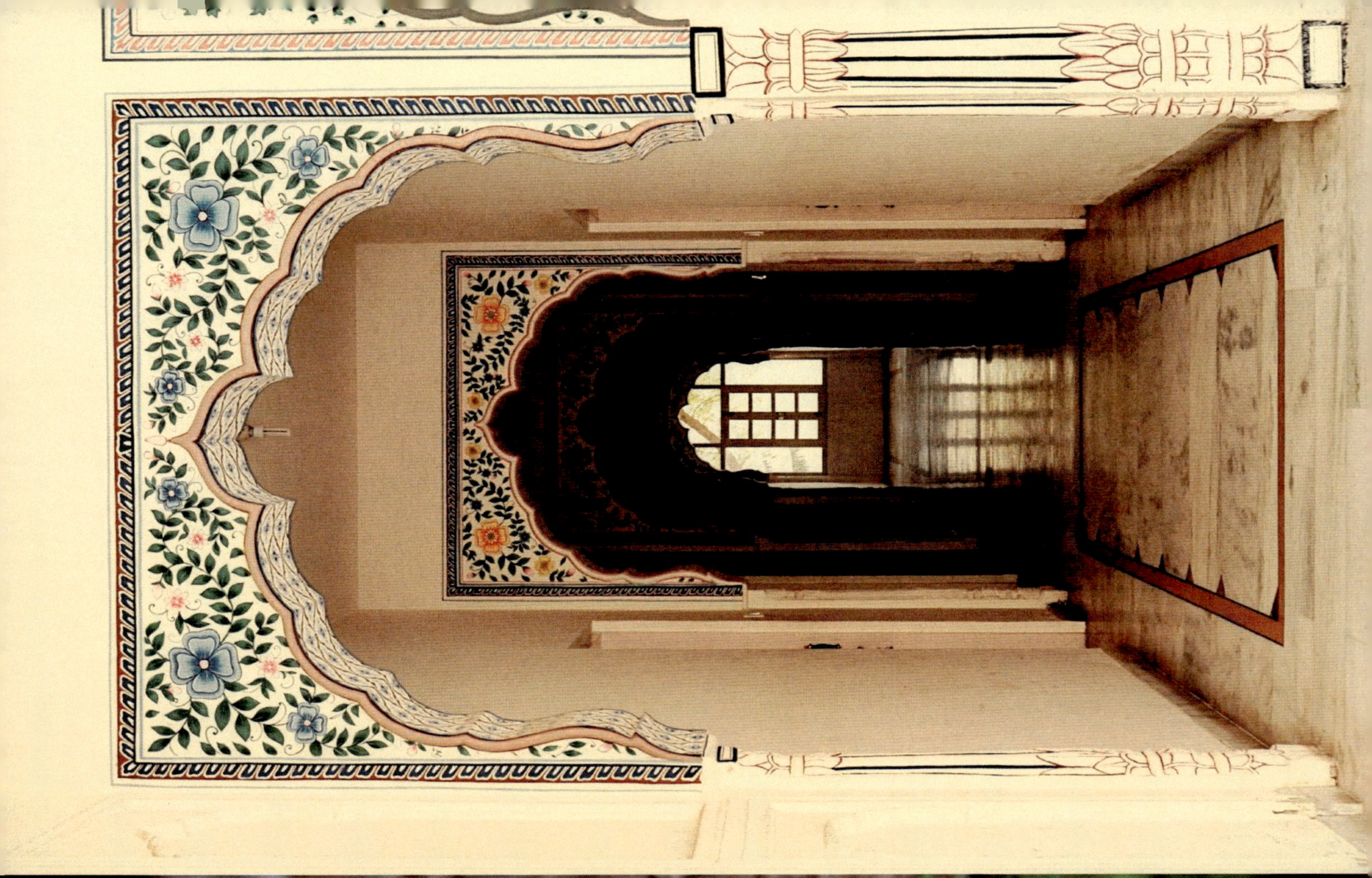

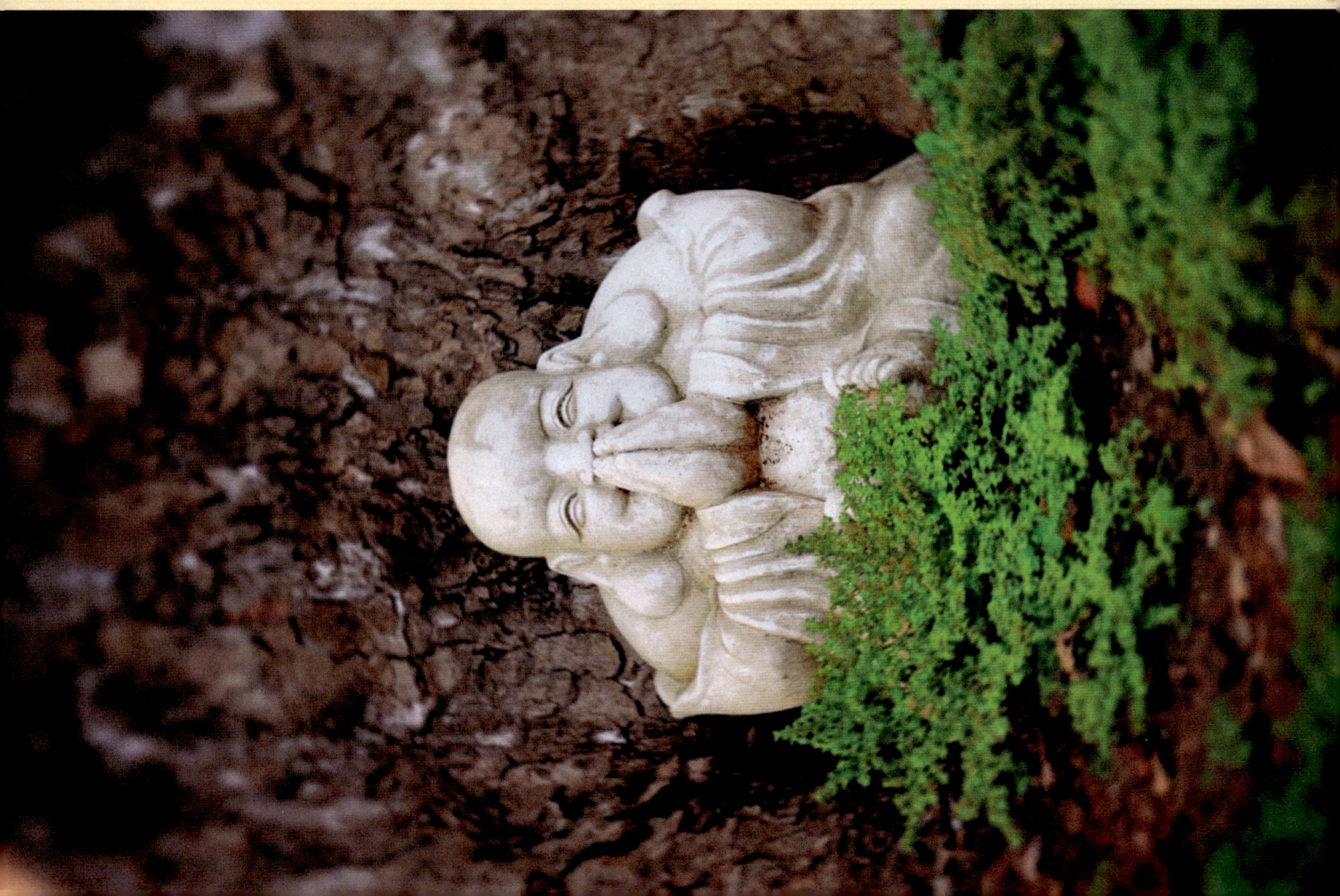

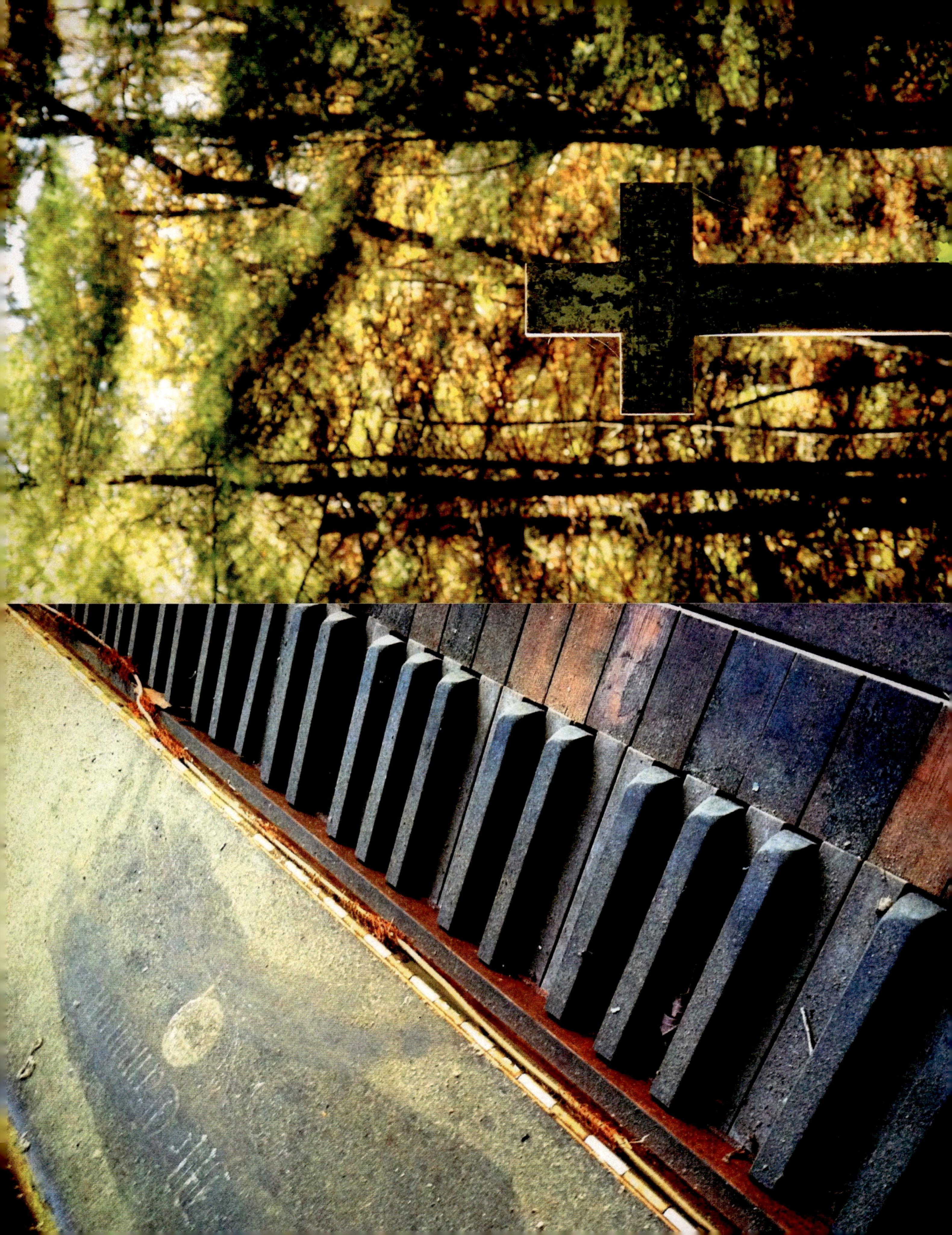

About Catherine

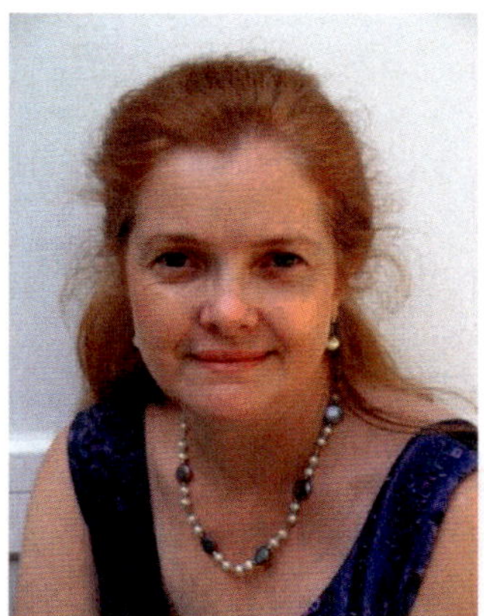

Catherine Anderson is author of *The Creative Photographer*, a book that combines inspiration, instruction and hands-on exercises to guide you in taking your photography to a more creative level. In addition the book gives you many ways to share your images through the use of mixed-media processes.

In 2004 Catherine trained as a SoulCollage® Facilitator with Seena Frost, the originator of the SoulCollage® process. Catherine is a SoulCollage® Facilitator Trainer, training others as Facilitators so they may share this transformational collage process throughout the world. Visit www.soulcollage.com for more information.

In addition, Catherine offers creative photography workshops and retreats in the US, Italy, France and South Africa. Her focus is on using photography as a way to slow down and see the world in a new way, and her online workshop *Seeing with Quiet Eyes: Photography as Meditative Practice* is a gentle introduction to this way of seeing.

The labyrinth is another of Catherine's passions and she has a labyrinth in her backyard, which she walks as a way to center and slow down. Catherine loves to share all her passions in her creativity workshops and encourage others to find their creative wings.

For more information, visit Catherine's website
www.catherineandersonstudio.com

The Creative Photographer is available through www.amazon.com

Made in the USA
Middletown, DE
06 September 2019